William Howard Merrell

Five Months in Rebeldom

Notes From the Diary of a Bull Run Prisoner, at Richmond

William Howard Merrell

Five Months in Rebeldom
Notes From the Diary of a Bull Run Prisoner, at Richmond

ISBN/EAN: 9783744761376

Printed in Europe, USA, Canada, Australia, Japan

Cover: Foto ©ninafisch / pixelio.de

More available books at **www.hansebooks.com**

FIVE MONTHS

IN

REBELDOM;

OR

NOTES FROM THE

DIARY OF A BULL RUN PRISONER,

AT RICHMOND.

———◆———

BY CORPORAL W. H. MERRELL,

Color Guard, Co. E., 27th Regiment, N. Y. S. V.

———◆———

ROCHESTER, N. Y.:
PUBLISHED BY ADAMS & DABNEY.
1862.

C. D. TRACY & CO., Printers, Rochester, N. Y.   J. LENNOX, Stereotyper.

INTRODUCTORY.

THE greater portion of the following narrative originally appeared in the columns of the ROCHESTER EVENING EXPRESS, in a series of twelve numbers. It was written at the request of the editors of that journal, of which Corporal Merrell had been a regular correspondent from the date of his enlistment till his release from Prison No. 1, in Richmond—comprising a period of nine months.

This narrative being the only full, consecutive and authentic account of prison life in Richmond, was widely copied by the Northern press, and eagerly sought by the public. During the progress of its original publication numerous requests were made for its reproduction in an enlarged and completed form, and Corporal M. being required to rejoin his regiment, was compelled to confide the work to the care and direction of a friend, by whom it is now presented in a form convenient for preservation and reference.

The incidents embodied in the narrative have at least the merit of novelty, few, if any of them, having been previously published; and it may be observed that most of them have been fully substantiated by the voluntary testimony of several of the fellow prisoners of Corporal Merrell, recently released. Indeed, the truth of one incident, of a peculiarly "romantic" character—and so much so as to have excited the incredulity of some readers—has been publicly endorsed in a letter over the signature of a brother of the prisoner to whom it personally relates.

The engraving of the Richmond "Prison No. 1," "Hospital No. 2," and the "Confederate Guard Quarters," which appears on a preceding page, is from a drawing by Corporal Merrell, and faithfully represents the Tobacco Warehouse in which the Union Officers, Civilians and many of the Privates were confined—(vide chap. v, p. 25.)

It is gratifying to know that the Government has finally inaugurated a system of "exchange" with the rebels. It, however, came too late to save or benefit many a patriotic, but unfortunate prisoner, who fell a victim to the neglect and cruelty of his rebel keepers. The fortitude exhibited by the captives under these unprecedented trials and privations, demonstrated a stern and unflinching loyalty, which is alike creditable to themselves and to the cause and the people for whom they have suffered. Their faith in the Union is still unshaken; their devotion to the "Stars and Stripes" is as pure and stedfast as ever, and no better evidence of this could be given than the fact that, generally, they have not only declined to accept a discharge from the service, but manifest a joyful alacrity in rejoining their comrades in arms, to enrol themselves under the now *advancing* and *conquering* banners of the Republic.

ROCHESTER, Feb. 1862.   W. W. B.

FIVE MONTHS IN REBELDOM;

OR

NOTES FROM THE DIARY OF A BULL RUN PRISONER.

CHAPTER I.

In compliance with the request of friends in Rochester, and in pursuance of a resolution previously formed, I propose to publish a few reminiscences of my involuntary sojourn in the "Old Dominion."

The events which I am to narrate are of so recent occurrence, that a retentive memory would suffice to recall them with all due exactness and circumstantiality; but were it otherwise, I have only to turn to a little pocket diary, which has been a faithful and indelible reflector of all important occurrences, as they transpired, during a five months' imprisonment in the Rebel Capital.

In presenting this narrative, I claim for it nothing but TRUTH-FULNESS—"a plain, unvarnished tale," wherein I shall

"Nothing extenuate, nor set down aught in malice;"

and may safely appeal to my late prison associates for the confirmation of any statement that is likely to be called in question.

With a view to form a connected narrative, I shall relate events in the order in which they transpired, commencing with my personal observations at the battle of Bull Run; yet, as it is no part of my design to describe that memorable engagement, I shall wholly confine myself to facts and incidents relating to my own regiment, the 27th N. Y. S. V. This regiment was organized at the Elmira Rendezvous in the month of May, and was ordered to Washington on the 10th of July. It consisted of three companies from Binghamton, one from Rochester, one from Albion, one from Lyons, one from Lima, one from Angelica, one from White Plains, and one from Mt. Morris. The field officers were Col. H. W. Slocum of Syracuse, Lt. Col. J. J. Chambers of White Plains, and Maj. J. J. Bartlett of Binghamton. The regiment had the reputation of being one of the best officered in the service, and notwithstanding that it was newly recruited and but partially inured to the hardships of camp life, it was believed to be as effectually disciplined as any volunteer corps in the army of the Potomac.

The 27th did not participate in the action of Thursday the 18th of July, but in that of the Sunday following their mettle was fully tested, and I believe that no impartial eye-witness of the battle of Bull Run will maintain that any regiment, whether regular or volunteer, exhibited a greater degree of gallantry on the field, manœuvered with better regularity or precision, were more exposed to the enemy's fire, or *suffered more severely* from its effects, than the one which had been facetiously christened the "Mutual Admiration Society" of Elmira. Notwithstanding the unaccustomed fatigues of an early and protracted march on Sunday morning, the feeling of the troops was animated, and they literally went on their way rejoicing. The enemy seemed hastily to abandon every position as we advanced, and the fact that the progress of the Union army from Washington had been marked only by a succession of light skirmishes, the less reflecting felt assured that we should not encounter a sufficient resistance on the way to Manassas, or even to Richmond, to furnish an appetite for rations. Yet how sadly different was the result.

Glancing back upon the interminable line of the Grand Army, as its several columns crept gradually toward Centerville—the sunlight flashing upon the serried bayonets, the regimental banners fluttering in the morning breeze, and the huge masses moving steadily, noiselessly and with the beautiful regularity of a street parade—the view was grand and imposing in the extreme, and though momentary, seemed worth the sight-seeing experiences of an entire life. But the eventful scenes were to come, and the predictions of those who assumed that the enemy were disposed to let us "onward to Richmond" without contesting our ability to force a passage, were speedily silenced by the sound of heavy artillery from the batteries to which we had been lured. There was no longer doubting the fact that we were approaching the field of battle. The roar of cannon was succeeded by the roll of musketry, which at every step became more and more audible, and it was easy to perceive that though not with us, yet elsewhere the work of carnage and of death had already commenced in earnest.

As I before intimated, I shall attempt no general description of the engagement, but rather confine myself in this connection to a narrative of events, as they transpired, in my immediate vicinity, and within the scope of my own observation.

It was my good fortune to be selected as one of the color-guard of the 27th. Soon after entering the field, we saw at a distance what appeared to be our National Flag, but which was in reality that of the enemy. While we were still in doubt, but advancing, Adjutant Jenkins rode forward, with the remark that he would soon determine whether they were friends or foes. He placed his havelock on the point of his sword, which he held aloft as a flag of truce, but as he approached them he was greeted with a volley of musketry. Unharmed, however, he rode quickly back to his regiment, exclaiming, with considerable emphasis, "Give 'em ——, boys." The 27th responded by opening their *hottest*(*!*) fire, and the enemy scattered. We subsequently learned that they were the 27th Virginia volunteers.

We continued to advance till confronted by the 8th Georgia, who stood their ground manfully for a time, loading and firing with great rapidity. They could not, however, withstand the regular and accurate discharges of the 27th, and we finally drove them back to a considerable distance, where they were reinforced. We were then in turn repulsed, and took refuge under a hill, where we remained until another advance was ordered.

[It was while resting here that one of my comrades, William Hanlon, of Rochester, company E, was most severely wounded. He was struck in the right leg by a cannon ball, and was thought to be killed outright. He survived, however, a cripple, to become a prisoner at Richmond, and was released and sent home on the 6th of October.]

Soon after this event Col. Slocum, our gallant commander, was ordered to charge a battery stationed on a knoll at our left, and was fearlessly leading on his regiment, in the midst of a tremendous fire, when he fell, severely wounded, and was immediately taken from the field. This occurrence was a severe blow to the regiment, who regarded their brave commander with a feeling of boundless affection. Happily he was spared to receive the appointment of Brigadier General, and the 27th is still under his charge.

The first member of the color-guard who was "struck" was Corporal Fairchild. The regiment had for a moment halted, when the Corporal staggered back, crying, "O, boys, I am struck!" Placing his hand upon his breast, with the expectation, as he afterwards said, of finding it "covered with blood," he accidentally felt the ball (a grapeshot) in his shirt pocket! He immediately pulled it out, exclaiming, "Thank God, I am safe!" It was a *spent ball*. The Corporal survived the battle to become a prisoner at Richmond.

In the meantime the action had become fierce and sanguinary, and every soldier in the ranks realized that his regiment was quite as severely "exposed" as the most ardent-minded and valorous could desire. Our numbers were greatly diminished, and though our discharges were rapid, they had become irregular, and the men loaded and fired promiscuously. An incident may be related in this connection of rather a novel character. Corporal S———n, of Rochester, a young man, who, since his enlistment, had been somewhat distinguished among his comrades for a religious zeal, fought manfully and with the "full assurance of faith." With every load of his musket he uttered an audible prayer to this effect: "O, Lord, send this bullet to the heart of a rebel, and *spare my life!*" A Manxman, who stood beside him, and who was quite as energetically engaged in the "discharge" of duty, censoriously retorted: "Hoot, mon—shoot more and pray less!" Shooting was evidently the most pressing business in hand, but our Manxman was probably not aware that a Yankee seldom attempts to do one thing at a time, and that it was quite proper to put two irons in the fire when the conflagration was so general and so extensive.

The 27th Regiment continued to march unflinchingly forward, literally amid a storm of "leaden rain and iron hail." Indeed, it seemed as though we were confronting an avalanche of bullets. Many were mowed down. I think that but one of our line officers then deserted his post of duty, and a few days since I met him in the streets of Rochester, wearing the uniform of a private. To my inquiries upon this subject, he admitted that he had been cashiered in consequence of his behavior on that occasion, and that he afterward returned home. "But," said he, "I could not help it; I ran despite of myself, for we were marching into the jaws of death. I am not a coward, and I mean to prove it. Therefore I have enlisted as a private soldier, and if I ever participate in another battle, I mean to stand my ground!"

In less than half an hour after the fall of General Slocum, the ranks of the color-guard were reduced from nine to two. The colors were large and weighty, and Sergeant Freeman having become quite exhausted, and myself too much so to relieve him, Major (now Colonel) Bartlett, who perceived the situation of affairs, came to our assistance. Riding along the line, and waving the colors above his head, he shouted, "Boys, will you fight for this?" The response was general and enthusiastic.

A large number of the enemy were discovered in the front, and the 27th advanced towards them, Sergeant Freeman being again in possession of the colors. At this conjuncture, while my piece was leveled, I received a ball in my breast and fell, remarking to my comrade that I should have to leave him. The Sergeant gave me a glance so full of sympathy at my misfortune that I never can forget it, and with the regiment passed on to meet the enemy. I crept to a rail fence near by, and lay insensible about fifteen or twenty minutes, as I should judge, and upon regaining consciousness, discovered that I was surrounded by numbers of dead and wounded. The immediate vicinity was not then occupied by troops. The first notable object that excited my attention was a Union soldier, who was wounded in the left arm, which lay powerless at his side. He was standing beside the fence, his piece resting upon the rail, and which, after taking deliberate aim, he discharged at the enemy. He then dropped his musket, and came and laid down beside me. No more passed between us, but I imagined he had obtained "satisfaction" for his own grievances.

While still lying in my position, I beheld another Union soldier at a short distance, climbing the fence. He held his musket in his right hand, but while astride of the fence, and in the act of getting down, a cannon-shot *struck the rail*, shattering it in pieces, and sending its rider whirling and summersetting in the air, with a velocity that would have astonished the most accomplished acrobat. He gathered himself up with almost an equal degree of alacrity, and started on "double quick" toward our own forces. He had proceeded but a few feet, however, when he came to a halt. Casting his eyes over his shoulder and perceiving that he was unpursued, he scratched his head thoughtfully for a moment, and then ran back and recovered his musket and started again for his regiment. I was in too much pain and bewilderment at the time to fully appreciate the comicality of this performance, but have since enjoyed many a hearty chuckle upon its reflection.

There was a great deal of skirmishing upon the field, and many instances of personal bravery particularly worthy of remark. I noticed, for example, one soldier leave his regiment, and crossing the field and leaping the fence, load and fire several times at a squad of cavalry. He was finally discovered, and three or four of their number rode down upon him. One who was in advance of the rest, came upon "our hero" as he was in the act of loading. He had driven the ball home, but had not withdrawn the ramrod. The horseman raised his sabre, and the next instant, as it appeared to me, the volunteer was to be short by a head; but suddenly inverting his musket, he dropped out the ramrod, and in the twinkling of an eye emptied the saddle and started back to his regiment. After proceeding a few rods, and finding that the enemy had given up the chase, he started back to recover his ramrod, and with it returned in triumph to his regiment, where he was greeted with rousing cheers.

But it is needless to multiply instances of this nature, so many of which have been already published by the press. The movements upon the field had in the meantime changed in such a manner that I found the spot where I lay exposed to the cross-firing, and accordingly crept to the cellar of "the old stone house." The passage was not unattended with danger, the rebels making a target of every living object upon that section of the field, (from which our troops had retreated,) and their balls whizzed briskly about me. The cellar in which I found refuge was already occupied by many other wounded Union soldiers, who had likewise sought its shel-

ter. They were lying in the mud and water upon the ground.
Upon entering, I discovered Corporal Fairchild, (above mentioned,
of the 27th,) who was moving about among the wounded, exerting
himself to relieve their sufferings by stanching their wounds, etc.
Their distracted and agonizing cries would have moved the most
obdurate heart to pity. "Water, water!" was the prayer upon
every tongue, but it was unavailing. To linger upon such a scene
is to recall one of the most painful experiences of my life, and one
which no words can adequately depict. The floor above was also
covered with wounded soldiers, whose cries could be distinctly
heard. I was not then aware that my friends and comrades, Clague
and Hanlon, of Rochester, were among the occupants of the upper
floor.

The cross-firing of the troops continued, and the rattle of musket balls against the walls of the building was almost incessant.
A number of them entered the windows, wounding three of the
inmates.

A cannon-shot also passed through the building, but inflicted
no bodily injury. Pending these occurrences, two rebel soldiers
entered the cellar, one of them seeking shelter in the fire-place.
They were both unwounded. The occupant of the fire-place, however, had not fairly ensconced himself when a musket ball passed
through his leg. The other, who was lying by my side, was also
severely wounded—a fitting penalty for their cowardice and de-
sertion.

Finding that the building was likely to be destroyed by the continued firing, one of our number went to the door, and placing a
havelock on his bayonet waved it aloft in the air. This *hospital
signal* was greeted with a shower of balls from the *Confederates*,
and he was compelled to retire. Subsequently a *yellow* flag was
displayed from the floor above, but it was likewise disregarded.

The wounded were perishing with thirst. At the distance of
about two rods from the building was a pump, and one noble fellow (whose name I regret that I have forgotten) took two canteens
and went out to obtain water. While so doing he received *five or
six musket balls*, in different portions of his body, from the rebel
forces—yet was not fatally injured. Though very low he was
still alive, an inmate of prison hospital No. 2, when I left Richmond. He will ever be remembered with gratitude and affection
by those who witnessed his noble conduct, and shared in the benefits of his exploit. It is my opinion that between fifty and sixty
men fell in the immediate vicinity of the pump and "the old stone
house."

From the position in which I lay, glancing outward, I could
discover the movements of troops upon the field, and at times
with tolerable distinctness. The battle seemed general, but irreg-

ular, and I witnessed no bayonet charges, or murderous hand-to-hand conflicts. The thrilling pictures by " our special artist, taken upon the spot," subsequently to adorn the pages of our enterprising illustrated weeklies, must have been seen "through a glass, darkly," or in the heated imaginations of that ubiquitous class of correspondents who simultaneously indite at Hong Kong, Constantinople and Salt Lake City, and invariably reach the sanctum in time to read the proof of their own missives.

The observations and impressions of another spectator of the same field, are thus truthfully and graphically described:

I'll tell you what I heard that day:
I heard the great guns, far away,
Boom after boom. Their sullen sound
Shook all the shuddering air around.

"What saw I?" Little. Clouds of dust;
Great squares of men, with standards thrust
Against their course; dense columns crowned
With billowing steel. Then, bound on bound,
The long black lines of cannon poured
Behind the horses, streaked and gored
With sweaty speed. Anon shot by,
Like a lone meteor of the sky,
A single horseman; and he shone
His bright face on me, and was gone.
All these, with rolling drums, with cheers,
With songs familiar to my ears,
Passed under the far hanging cloud,
And vanished, and my heart was proud!

At length a solemn stillness fell
Upon the land. O'er hill and dell
Failed every sound. My heart stood still,
Waiting before some coming ill.
The silence was more sad and dread,
Under that canopy of lead,
Than the wild tumult of the war
That raged a little while before.
All nature, in her work of death,
Paused for one last, despairing breath;
And, cowering to the earth, I drew
From her strong breast, my strength anew.

When I arose, I wondering saw
Another dusty vapor draw,
From the far right, its sluggish way
Towards the main cloud, that frowning lay
Against the westward sloping sun;
And all the war was re-begun,
Ere this fresh marvel of my sense
Caught from my mind significance.
O happy dead, who early fell,
Ye have no wretched tale to tell

Of causeless fear and coward flight,
Of victory snatched beneath your sight,
Of martial strength and honor lost,
Of mere life bought at any cost.
Ye perished in your conscious pride,
Ere this misfortune opened wide
A wound that cannot close or heal
Ye perished steel to levelled steel,
Stern votaries of the god of war,
Filled with his godhead to the core!

While our forces were on the retreat, pursued by the rebels, a body of troops halted at the stone building, entered with bayonets, and demanded a surrender! They were to all appearances as much intimidated as though they had anticipated a successful resistance. None was made, however. No violence was offered to the prisoners, and in this connection, I may state that I saw no "bayoneting" whatever committed by the enemy at Bull Run. Our arms were delivered up, and a few moments afterward I was led and half-carried away to the quarters of Gen. Beauregard, situate at a distance of perhaps half a mile. Before reaching there, we encountered Gen. Beauregard, flanked by Johnson and Davis, riding across the field. Their countenances were illuminated with a mingled feeling of joy and exultation, and they could well afford, as they did, to salute an unfortunate prisoner. The head-quarters consisted of a large white house. It was filled with wounded soldiers, undergoing surgical attention. Fragments of human bodies were strewed upon the verandah and about the building, and large numbers of both Union and rebel wounded lay outside upon the ground.

On arriving at head-quarters, my guard, who was a private soldier, pointed me out to a "Louisiana Tiger," and performed the ceremony of introduction by saying, "Here's one of our Tigers!"—and—"Here's a d—d Yankee!" I expected a savage growl, not to say the roughest of embraces at the hands of the savage forester, and was not a little surprised when he approached me kindly, with the remark, "Are you wounded, sir?" I replied in the affirmative, when he resumed, "I am sorry for you. I hope you will soon recover, and be restored to your friends." My companion, the guard, appeared to be quite as much astonished as myself; though less agreeably so, I have no doubt.

The case above noted may have been exceptional, for I was afterwards subjected to frequent insults from private soldiers, though kindly treated, in general, by the "Confederate" officers.

Night closed in with a pouring rain, and the wounded lay upon the ground unsheltered. I slept soundly, after these unaccustomed hardships, and was awakened by the sound of the morning *reveille.* My arm was stiff, my wound extremely painful, and my physical powers quite exhausted. A Lieutenant approached me and inquired as to my condition, and I begged him to find me a shelter. He absented himself for a short time, and then returned to say that there was but one place to be had, and that was a tent which was already filled with Confederate wounded, but that if I was content to lay in the water for the sake of a shelter overhead, he would try to provide for me. I gladly accepted the offer, and soon found myself at the place indicated. As I entered, a wounded Confederate soldier, who had a blanket above and another beneath him, offered me one of them, which I at first politely declined. He however insisted, and I was soon enjoying its protection. Soon after, I observed a young man standing at the opening of the tent and looking within. As he glanced at me I nodded, and stooping down he kindly inquired if he could do anything to relieve me. After some conversation, I gave him the address of my wife, begging him to write and inform her of my misfortune, etc. He was, it appeared, a Methodist student, and though a private soldier in the ranks of the rebels, was then acting in the capacity of Chaplain, and administering consolation to the wounded. I should occupy too much space in reporting our discussions at length. Before leaving, he kneeled in the water at my side and offered one of the most eloquent and moving supplications to which I have ever listened. He soon after fulfilled his promise to notify my family of my condition, and subsequently, during my imprisonment, called upon me and placed in my hand five dollars and a copy of the Bible. I shall ever treasure it as a memento of our brief acquaintance, and of my heartfelt gratitude toward William E. Boggs, of Wainsboro, South Carolina.

CHAPTER II.

While I was lying in the tent of the wounded "Confederates," a private soldier who had just received his ration, (consisting of half a pint of coffee, a hard biscuit and a small piece of bacon,) brought it to me, saying, " You need this more than I do." I at first hesitated to accept it, but he urged it upon me, remarking, " We were enemies yesterday, in the field, but we are friends to-day, in misfortune."

I would again state that these are exceptional instances of the feeling generally manifested by the rebels toward their prisoners, and the fact rather enhances my feeling of gratitude for the kind-hearted treatment, of which, at times, I was so singularly the recipient.

While the above scene was transpiring, a number of officers were standing near, conversing, and one of them asked me how it was that men who fought so bravely could retreat, when the day was fairly *their own?* The speaker said it was at first believed to be a "Yankee trick," or the Confederates would have followed up their advantage! He solicited my opinion on this subject, and I assured him (of what I fully believed,) that our forces would unquestionably return, and quite as unexpectedly as they had retired.

I was soon informed that all of the prisoners whose condition was such as to withstand the fatigues of the journey, would be immediately removed to Manassas; and soon after I was placed in a lumber wagon, beside one other prisoner and three wounded rebels, and we reached our destination after about an hour's drive through a forest road. It struck me as rather significant that the direct road was avoided, and hence no prisoner transported in this manner was afforded an inspection of the enemy's defenses.

The rain continued to pour in torrents, and without intermission. As we arrived opposite the depot at Manassas, I was afforded a glimpse of the place. The most prominent was the hospital, a large frame structure, opposite to which was the only battery to be seen in the vicinity. The only mounted piece was a shell-mortar. There were perhaps a dozen small frame buildings, which comprised the "Junction" proper. All of these seemed to have been appropriated to the accommodation of the Confederate wounded. Numerous tents had been pitched for a similar purpose, and temporary sheds were also in process of erection.

The Confederates were assisted from the wagon; my fellow-prisoner also descended and went off to obtain shelter, and even the guard and driver, thoroughly drowned out by the deluge, deserted their posts of duty, and left me to

"Bide the pelting of the pitiless storm"

in solitude. I finally managed to get out upon the ground, and crept along, "swimmingly," to the hospital. There I was refused admission, on account of its over-crowded state, but finally prevailed upon the steward to let me within the hall, where with a number of others, I remained for about one hour. As formerly, when I had reached almost the *lowest* depth of despondency, I was so fortunate as to secure a friend in a wounded rebel soldier. In the course of our conversation, he informed me that all of the prisoners were to be conveyed to Richmond. He was going as far as Culpepper, where his parents resided, and he assured me that if I desired to go with him, I should receive the best of medical care and attention. I accepted the kind offer conditionally, as I did not wish to be separated from my wounded comrades. He then—upon receiving my parole of honor—assumed the responsibility of my custody, and we were soon among the passengers of a crowded train, and speeding "on to Richmond."

The journey occupied two days, the train being required to halt at every station from one to three hours. All along the route great crowds of people were assembled, consisting mostly of women and children, and at almost every place large numbers of Confederate wounded were removed from the cars, followed by weeping and distracted relatives. Some of these scenes were very affecting.

Davis, Lee, and other Confederate magnates, accompanied us as far as Orange Court House, and at intervening points the first named was called out upon the platform to speak to the multitudes. At some villages the women thronged about the cars, offering refreshments to the wounded, both Union and Confederate, but more particularly to the former, whom they seemed to regard with mingled curiosity and favor. I suspected that the sympathies of some were even more deeply enlisted than they dared to avow. We were invariably addressed as "Yankees," and there were frequent inquiries respecting "Old Scott, the traitor," and "Old Lincoln, the tyrant." The ladies generally expressed a benevolent desire to "get hold" of the hero of Lundy's Lane, in order to string him up.

Arriving at Culpepper, the daughter of Major Lee, a young and beautiful damsel, came up to the window from which I leaned, and asked if she could do anything for me; and added, "What did you come down here for?" [This had become a stereotyped query.] I replied, "To protect the Stars and Stripes and preserve the Union."

My questioner then proceeded, after the uniform custom, to berate Gen. Scott. "That miserable Old Scott—a Virginian by birth—a traitor to his own State—*we all hate him!*" And the heightened color, the vindictive glance and the emphatic tones of the excited maiden, furnished assurance that her anger was unfeigned. But it quickly subsided, and after some further conversation, she took from her bonnet a miniature silken secession flag, which she handed to me, remarking that she thought I could fight as well for the "Stars and Bars," as for the Stars and Stripes. I playfully reminded her that she had just denounced Gen. Scott as a traitor to his own State, and if I should fight for the "Stars and Bars," I should be a traitor to the State of New York! This trivial argument was evidently a poser. "Oh!" responded she, "I had not thought of that!"—But she insisted upon my acceptance of the emblem of disloyalty, and I still retain it as a memento of the occurrence, and with a feeling of kindly regard for the donor. She cut the buttons from my coat sleeve, and I consented to the "formal exchange," though not exactly recognizing her as a "belligerent power."

As Miss Lee retired, another young lady came forward, and glancing at my companion, the Confederate guard, addressed him as a "Yankee prisoner," expressing her indignant surprise that he should have invaded their soil to fight them. He corrected her mistake, stating that I, not he, was the "Yankee prisoner."

"No—no—you can't fool me; I know the Yankees too well," insisted the lady. I corroborated the assertion of my custodian, but it was some time before her prejudices could be overcome.

At almost every station on the route, one or more dead bodies were removed from the train, and placed in charge of their friends. The University at or near Culpepper, and the Church at Warrenton, had been fitted up for hospital purposes, and large numbers of the Confederate wounded were conveyed to them from the train. Of the six or seven cars which started from Manassas, there were but two remaining when we reached the rebel capital. We arrived there about 9 o'clock in the evening. After the cars*had halted, I heard a low voice at my window, which was partly raised. It was quite dark, and I could not distinguish the speaker, who was evidently an Irish woman.

"Whist, whist!" said she; "are ye hungry?"

I replied that I was not, but that some of the boys probably were.

"Wait till I go to the house," she answered, and a moment afterward I heard her again at the window. She handed me a loaf of bread, some meat, and about a dozen baker's cakes, saying—as she handed me the first—"That was all I had in the house, but I had a shillin', and I bought the cakes wid it; and if I had more, sure you should have it and welcome! Take it, and God bless ye!"

I thanked her, and said, "You are very kind to enemies."

"Whist," said she, "and *ain't I from New York meself?*" and with this tremulous utterance she retired as mysteriously as she had come.

This was the first "Union demonstration" that I witnessed in Old Virginia I thanked God for the consolation which the reflection afforded me, as for the third night I lay sleeplessly in the cars, my clothing still saturated and my body thoroughly chilled from the effects of the deluge at Manassas. I could have desired no sweeter morsel than the good woman's homely loaf; and proud of the loyal giver, I rejoiced that "I was from New York meself."

The following morning the prisoners were all removed to the hospital and provided with comfortable quarters and medical attendance.

CHAPTER III.

The Military Hospital is a large brick structure, in the form of the letter E, without the middle bracket. It is pleasantly located on a slight elevation in the northern suburbs of the city, and near the fortifications commanding the entrance from Manassas. It was originally designed for a poor-house, and had not reached a completed state when it was required for hospital purposes. The car load of wounded with whom I arrived, constituted the first instalment of hospital inmates, and, as before stated, we were immediately provided with comfortable quarters, and for the first time since the battle had our wounds dressed. Upon every succeeding day we received numerous accessions to our number, until the hospital was filled to its utmost capacity. Indeed, the floors were covered with cots, and every available space was occupied by the form of a wounded Union soldier. The head-Surgeon of the establishment was Dr. Peachy, of Richmond. He had a numerous corps of assistants, consisting principally of medical students, who had gladly availed themselves of the opportunity to engage at once in an extensive, if *not* a successful practice. Dr. Peachy himself is an amiable, kind-hearted gentleman, whose sympathies seemed deeply enlisted in behalf of his unfortunate patients, and was untiring in his professional attentions, which were impartially distributed between officers and privates.

The Sisters of Charity of Richmond had volunteered their services in behalf of the wounded, and many a poor fellow would gladly testify to their kind and unremitting attentions—and how that

> The charities that soothe, that heal, that bless,
> Were scattered round his lowly couch like flowers.

Hardly were the prisoners comfortably bestowed in hospital quarters, before the place literally swarmed with visitors. The greater portion of them were ladies, who brought us dainties of every description, and in some instances articles of underclothing, which were greatly needed. It is undoubtedly the fact that the benevolence of many of these ladies was prompted by feelings of loyalty to the Federal Government, which in no other way could find a practical expression.

Among them was at least one, a lady of *the highest* social and political connections in Richmond, whose name (which I would

2

gladly publish) I am induced from prudential motives to withhold.   On the day of our arrival she visited the hospital, attended by a female companion and a negro servant, bearing baskets
generously laden with luxuries of every kind.   Her pockets, also,
were crammed with *plug tobacco* and cakes of castile soap, which
she clandestinely distributed among the patients.   To her kind-
ness and ingenuity I was indebted for the secret conveyance of
the first letter which I was enabled to write, and also the first, as
I was afterwards informed, which left Richmond from the prisoners taken at Bull Run.   The anxiety of this kind lady to more
fully relieve the distresses of the wounded prisoners, at length
overcame her discretion, and her work of benevolence was estop-
ped by a formal investigation.   It was argued by the hospital
authorities that the Confederate wounded were more properly the
subjects for the exercise of Southern benevolence, and that the
extravagant charities bestowed upon the "Yankees" were evidences of a "Union" sentiment that could not be tolerated without detriment to the "Confederacy."

The lady in question, as well as others, likewise generous,
were at length grossly assailed by the Richmond press, and afterwards prohibited from administering to our comfort, and finally were even refused admission to the hospital.   In this connection I may state that several of our lady visitors informed me
that they belonged in the North, but were compelled to remain in
Richmond.   It will be remembered that in Norfolk an order was
issued asking all "alien enemies," who desired to return North,
to report themselves at a given time to the Confederate authorities, and they would be then sent under a flag of truce to Fortress
Monroe.   As a result, a large number, who had succeeded in
evading suspicion, presented themselves at the place indicated,
where their names were registered.   But instead of being sent
to Fortress Monroe, they were arrested and sent to Richmond!
Here, of course, they were subjected to a system of *espionage* established by King Jeff. to promote the safety of his Confederate
despotism.   One lady, whose acquaintance I had made in the
hospital, informed me that the Stars and Stripes were concealed
in her house, and that she only waited a favorable opportunity to
fling them to the breeze!

I shall not dwell at length upon the painful and exciting scenes
which transpired under my notice at the hospital.   On the fourth
day after I entered that place, I was surprised at recognizing
my old comrade of the 27th, John F. Clague, who was brought in
with a large number of wounded.   This "batch" (to use the hospital term applied to new comers) comprised some of the most
critical cases brought from Manassas.   Many of them had been

picked up from the field two days after the battle, and their recovery was regarded as hopeless.

The amputating room was in the center of the building, within easy call of any part of the hospital, and the frightful cries of the unfortunate subjects, while undergoing surgical operation, added a ten-fold torture to the pangs of those who were in waiting. Upon the average, as the physicians estimated, but *one in ten* survived their amputations. Consequently, when one of our number was removed to the "amputating table," we felt that we looked upon him for the last time. These operations frequently lasted one or two hours, the patient being under the influence of chloroform and whisky. Frequently the subject survived several days, but always in great suffering.

Although many expressed a mortal dread of the terrible ordeal, there were others who submitted to it with a fortitude which seemed unexampled. In one instance a young man by the name of Farmer, from Minnesota, was twice compelled to submit to the amputation of his left leg. The first operation was performed at Manassas, but during his journey to Richmond the jolting of the cars inflamed the wound, and disarranged the bandages. Mortification ensued, and he was informed he must undergo a second operation. He received the announcement with a *cheerful smile*, and said that he was ready. Here, indeed, was the teaching of

"How sublime a thing it is to suffer and be strong."

The fearful ordeal was passed triumphantly, but he was replaced in his ward to *die*. The Confederate attendants, in passing through the hospital, frequently stopped to speak to him, and he always responded smilingly to their inquiries, that he was doing well and should recover. When asked if he did not regret having invaded their territory, he invariably answered: "No, no, he had nothing whatever to regret!"

With his comrades, however, he confessed that his sufferings were intense, and expressed doubts of his recovery. The last time I conversed with him, he requested a pipe of tobacco, which I procured for him, and left him tranquilly smoking in his cot and apparently enjoying his own reflections. In a little while he called me again to his side, and in the politest manner asked me to bring him some water, which I speedily obtained. A short time afterward I again approached his couch and discovered that *his face was covered*. He had indeed,

Passed through Glory's morning gate,
And walked in Paradise.

The only instance of brutality that I witnessed, occurred during an operation performed upon a Michigan Captain. His right thigh had been shattered by a minie ball, and required an amputation at the *hip*. Probably no severer operation is known in surgical practice. The subject was stupified with chloroform, and the sponge was constantly held to his nostrils; but his shrieks and groans were unintermitting, and agonizing in the extreme. During the operation, a rebel soldier employed in the hospital stood at his head, assisting to hold him down. His sense of the proprieties of the occasion could not tolerate the cries of the wretched victim, and he rudely told him to "stop his noise," and "shut his mouth." Not finding himself obeyed, the brutal fellow with great rudeness clasped, or rather struck, both of his palms over the Captain's face, and held them firmly there till discovered by one of the students, who then ordered him from the room. The operation was finally performed, the limb being disjointed at the hip. Three hours afterward the sufferer was relieved by death.

One other case of a totally different character may be noted. Upon one occasion a young man was borne into the hospital who represented that he had *seven bullets* in his body. His sufferings had excited much sympathy at Manassas, and upon removal he had to be carried to the cars on a litter. His groans drew tears of pity from even the Confederate guards, and every one who approached him expressed the opinion that it was the most shocking case that had appeared. He was handled with exceeding carefulness in being conveyed to the hospital, and immediately placed upon a cot, not, however, without extorting some of the most agonizing utterances to which I ever listened. Dr. Peachy soon approached him and inquired as to the nature of his wounds. "Seven bullets," was the laconic response. "But where are they?" continued the Doctor. "One of them went in my ear, and I feel it in my head," was the reply, "but you can't find it, and there's no use of trying."

As to the locality of the other wounds, he professed ignorance, with the exception of one, which he said had shattered his foot. The foot was examined, and the heel of it was found to be slightly contused. Finally, the sufferer confessed that this was the extent of his injuries. He said he had feared that unless dreadfully wounded he would be roughly treated, if not put to death, and had accordingly determined to resort to a Yankee trick. It was highly successful. He was immediately christened "Seven Bullets," and is known by no other title among his prison associates to this day.

CHAPTER IV.

Among the prisoners taken at Bull Run was Capt. Ricketts, of Rickett's Battery, Regular Army. He was severely wounded, and was removed with others to the General Hospital, where he was placed with the commissioned officers, in an apartment on the second floor. I introduce his name in this connection for the purpose of testifying to the devoted heroism of his affectionate wife, who, having heard of his misfortune, immediately proceeded from New York to Washington, and, unattended, made her way to the enemy's lines, and surrendered herself a prisoner, with the request that she might be permitted to attend her husband. Her application was granted, but while journeying from Manassas to Richmond, she was grossly insulted by the rebel soldiery, and encountered many formidable obstacles to the success of her mission. Her indomitable perseverance was, however, at length rewarded, and she obtained admission to the hospital, where she remained several months. Once there, her kindly attentions were not restricted to her husband, or to the officers' apartment, but in a little while she was known to all the inmates, and her cheering smiles and womanly sympathy were like gleams of sunshine upon every heart. When I was removed from the hospital she was still there, faithfully administering to the wants of the suffering and encouraging the desponding to hope for better days. There are none among the prisoners who can recall the name of Mrs. Fanny Ricketts without feelings of the deepest gratitude and brotherly affection.

Several of Ellsworth's Fire Zouaves were among the wounded, and I observed that they were regarded by the Confederate soldiers with a feeling of aversion which they were at no pains to conceal. One of their (the Zouaves') number was a young Virginian named Brown, who had long resided in New York. Shortly after his arrival at the hospital he was visited by his father, who is a resident of Richmond. The interview was not characterized by any display of tenderness on either side, but was one of those scenes, rather, which are best calculated to illustrate the implacable hatred with which the rebels regard *all* who have not proved faithless to the General Government. The father was a stubborn rebel and the son a PATRIOT SOLDIER. The scene may be better imagined than described. After exhausting every argument and expostulation upon the unrelenting boy, the old man *disowned*, and declared that he would disinherit him. To this the young soldier replied that his only hope was that he might recover from his wounds, get back to the Union army, and fight again for the Stars and Stripes! And thus they separated. The gallant soldier was among the released prisoners of the 3d of January, and upon placing his foot upon the Federal steamer was the very first to propose "three cheers for the Stars and Stripes." I regret to add that he is not yet fully recovered from his wounds, and was at last accounts confined in the military hospital at Baltimore.

I had been three weeks in the Richmond hospital when a large number of the patients were transferred to one of the tobacco warehouses, and their places refilled by Confederate soldiers, who were suffering from measles, typhoid fever and other diseases. They had been sent from the hospital at Manassas. No pains were taken to separate this class of patients from the Federal wounded, and it is not a little strange that these diseases, known to be infectious, were not communicated to other inmates.

This new fellowship was not particularly inviting, and the wounded generally reserved their sympathies for mutual exchange—assisting one another so far as practicable, and enjoying their little luxuries in common. By degrees, however, the new companionship ripened into familiar intercourse, and then came political discussions, which at times provoked considerable ill-feeling on both sides. All were *uncompromising* in their opinions, and the debates frequently terminated in the most emphatic and war-like declarations. At such times the excitement usually found vent in fist-shaking, and other threatening gestures, but upon one occasion, a prisoner gravely proposed that an equal number should be chosen from each side, of all that were able to *walk*, and who should go into the hospital yard and settle their contentions by a fair fight! The rebels would not, however, accede to this proposition, and thenceforth the Federalists regarded the question of our relative manhood and bravery as practically settled.

The fact of the matter was, (and I say it not in a boastful spirit,) that the rebels only desired to be let alone! It was the head and tail of their every argument. "Why do you come here to subjugate us?—Let us alone. We want peace—*let us alone!* We have done nothing—LET US ALONE!"

One of their number approached me—and he is the type of a *very* numerous class—and asked me with all candor if *I* knew what the South was fighting *for?* I told him what every soldier in the army of the Union knows. He was of the opinion that they were acting solely in self-defence; that the North, or Lincoln, had deliberately commenced the war with a view to subjugate the South, desolate their homes, liberate their slaves, insult their women—and all this chiefly that we might enrich ourselves, and gratify a feeling of wanton malice against our "Southern brethren!" And these opinions, religiously cherished, he assured me were largely shared by the Confederate army. Yet with all their gullibility they have a latent suspicion of the open-eyed conspiracy of which they were made the victims; and it was easy to perceive that there were many among them who had "no stomach for the fight." They had been literally impressed into the service of the Rebel Government and awaited only a favorable opportunity to desert.

I could give numerous instances in point, but select a single one as a matter of local interest. I was accosted one day by a private (rebel) soldier, who came to the hospital as a visitor. He inquired my place of residence, etc., and upon learning it informed me that he was from Utica, N. Y., and had been employed as clerk for Owen Gaffney, Esq., (now of Rochester.) He mentioned the names of many persons whom I knew, and finally informed me that although a soldier in the rebel army, he was there because he could not help himself, and was seeking an opportunity to escape.

Speaking of visitors, there were others worthy of notice, and among them the dapper Vice President of the bogus Confederacy, Mr. Alexander Stevens. There were a number of Georgians confined in the hospital, and Mr. Stevens had called to inquire after their welfare. He is a foppish little fellow, with long, straight hair and a beardless face, wears his hat at an acute angle, sports a switch cane and a Byron collar, and might be mistaken, at first glance, for a broken down theatre actor. I think he would probably turn the scale of 125 pounds, if he bore down very *hard*. He is of a reserved demeanor, quiet, unpretending and agreeable in conversation, and while talking with the prisoners seemed to studiously avoid any remark that could be supposed to injure their feelings. He visited us quite often.

We were also "honored" with a call from the editor of the Richmond Dispatch, who came in disguise, and regaled the prisoners with plug tobacco and cigars, professed the deepest sympathy, and was exceedingly inquisitive. The day following he spread before his readers an account of his observations at the hospital, wherein he took occasion to denounce us in the most unsparing terms. Tray, Blanche and Sweetheart joined in this demoniac *yowl*, and for a brief season little else was advocated by the Richmond press than a proposition to remove the "lazy Yankees" to the coal mines as soon as their wounds were healed, and compel them to work for their living. The editor of the Dispatch subsequently renewed his visit, and was recognized. The boys, however, professed to regard him as a stranger, but improved the opportunity to introduce the said editor as a topic of discussion, and berated him to their satisfaction. Believing himself unknown he bore it without remonstrance, but did not remain long, and we never "looked upon his like again."

We had visitors of every class. I was leaning upon the balcony one day, when an elderly lady approached me, saying that she desired to pass into the ward where the Confederate patients were confined, but she did not want to see any of the "horrid Yankees." I had understood that the popular superstition respecting Federal soldiers, savored of horns and claws; but not calculating the effect of a sudden avowal, I remarked, in winning accents and with the pleasantest distortion of countenance of which my facial muscles were susceptible, that I was a "beast of Ephesus" myself! The disclosure seemed to take effect in the lady's stomach, for after a tragic and momentary collapse which threatened to snap the spinal column, she wildly flung up her arms, exclaiming "O-YAH-UGH!" and vanished.

On every Sunday the outskirts of the prison were thronged with visitors, who had come upon a staring expedition, and seemed amply repaid if they obtained a glimpse of the Yankees. Barnum's Museum would have passed for a side-show, in comparison with the hospital attractions. Upon one occasion I was standing at the window with a companion, when we were accosted by a savage-looking fellow under a planter's hat, and very genteelly dressed, who asked me if I had had enough of Bull Run. I replied by inquiring if he was there. No—he was not. "I supposed not," said I, "for any one who would insult a prisoner is too cowardly to go where there is any danger."

I regretted the observation, for it was no sooner uttered than the prancing fire-eater emitted the most sulphurous volley of oaths that I had heard on the "sacred soil." Fuming and snorting with wrath he paced backward and forward, his glittering eye

"In a fine frenzy rolling,"

till having collected himself for a second attack, he exclaimed, "Well, you belong to the Confederates *now*—you are in *our power.*"

My companion asked him if *he* belonged to the Confederates? "Yes," he rejoined with emphasis, "*I do!*"

"Well, what does your master ask for you?" said the former.

This was a sad blow to the "chivalric" Southerner, who was of a suspiciously *dark complexion*, and certainly could not be classed among "poor white trash." To add to his discomfiture, the bystanders laughed as heartily as the "Yankees." The only resource of our rabid friend was to cast out another volley of oaths, but before he could do justice to his subject, he was walked off by the guard.

CHAPTER V.

The scarcity of lint, or plaster, was the most serious want experienced by the hospital surgeons, and at one period the supply was entirely cut off, and our wounds were for a time left undressed. "Tell your master, Lincoln, to raise the blockade, and then we will provide for you," was the frequent remark of the surgeons. "As it is, we haven't enough for our own wounded, and they must be served first." Cotton was substituted, and that article being a "drug" in the medical cabinet, it in point of *quantity* subserved the desired purpose.

On the 11th of September I was transferred from the general hospital to Prison No. 1—a tobacco warehouse, situate on the bank of the James river.* There were some half dozen tobacco factories appropriated to similar purposes, but my observations were necessarily restricted to the one in which I enjoyed a "personal interest." It is a lofty brick building, three stories in height, its interior dimensions being seventy feet in length by twenty-six in width. The second and third floors were occupied by private soldiers, (captured at Bull Run,) and the lower floor by the commissioned officers and a number of civilians, among whom were our late lamented fellow-citizen, Calvin Huson, Jr., Esq., and the Hon. Alfred Ely.

The windows of the third story commanded an excellent view of the city and its environs, but from the lower floor little was to be seen, beyond the street boundaries. I was placed in the department occupied by the privates. It was in a most crowded state, as may be inferred from the fact that at no time were there less than one hundred and thirty, and often as many as one hundred and fifty occupants. There were no artificial conveniences for either eating or sleeping. At night the prisoners stretched themselves upon the bare floor, uncovered; and at meal time—if the irregular and melancholy farce of *eating* may be thus interpreted—they sat upon the floor, ranging against the walls, and (in primitive style) devoured whatever they could obtain.

A more gloomy and revolting spectacle can hardly present itself to the imagination, than was afforded by these filthy quarters. Let the reader picture a hundred haggard faces and emaciated forms—some with hair and beard of three months growth—so miserably clothed, in general, as scarcely to subserve the purposes of decency; and many limping about with pain from healed wounds;

---
*See engraving.

and then some faint conception may be obtained of the wretched condition of these Union prisoners. I have still in my possession a note which I received from one of my comrades (an inmate of this prison), while I was still in the hospital. It reads as follows:

TOBACCO WAREHOUSE, August 25, 1861.

DEAR MERRELL: Have you got or can you get us a shirt or two and a pair of drawers? I am almost entirely naked. The shirt I have on, I have worn for three weeks. It was very much torn when I put it on, and now it is all in ribbons. My woolen shirt, drawers and a pair of stockings are all somewhere in the hospital. I don't suppose you can find them, but if you possibly can, *do* send at least a shirt, if no more. If you can't, heaven only knows what will become of me. I am very much in need of a towel, also.

My wound is getting along well—indeed, I am getting stronger. There are quite a number of our regiment here, but none from our company. Please give my kindest regards to Sister Rose, and tell her I most heartily wish myself back under her care.   J.

P. S.—If you can get a piece of corn bread, send that along, too. We don't see any of that article in these parts.

The condition above described was characteristic of a large portion of the prisoners; yet there were many whose privations were even worse. The prison discipline was as follows: Between eight and nine we received our morning ration, which consisted of bread (half baked), beef and water. The individual allowance was in quantity about *one-half* what a well man would naturally require. Our second and only other ration was received between four and five in the afternoon, and consisted of bread and soup—(the beef dispensed in the morning being taken from the "slops" of the day previous.) This was the standard bill of fare. The prisoners, sick and well, were compelled to accept it or—go without.

A few of our number had blankets, and some of these were sold to the guard, and the avails appropriated to the purchase of edibles which could not be otherwise procured.

The "poetasters" of Prison No. 2 could not resist the impulse to immortalize our "Prison Bill of Fare," and a concentrated effort at versification resulted in the following production, the authorship of which I believe is claimed by Sergeant Solomon Wood, of the 27th Regiment. I extract the more significant portions:

First, at the sink having performed ablution,
The problem, "*what's for breakfast?*" needs solution.
Like others not in Euclid, oft 'tis found
To tax researches that are most profound.
At length 'tis solved, when on his sapient head
A colored gemman brings a loaf of bread,—
Not common loaves, as in the shop you'll find,
Such large affairs must suit the vulgar mind.
Our friends take care our better tastes to meet,
So send us loaves that are unique and neat;

Our longing eyes upon the batch we fix,
Then quickly eat our rations,—ounces six;
So justly are our appetites defined,
These loaves are not the largest of their kind;
To season them withal, our friends allow
Three ounces of some lately butchered cow;
How long ago we say not, but the smell
Would indicate it rather hard to tell;
The doubt, however, is not worth discussing,
Such things create unnecessary fussing;
Besides, it would be wrong to heed such stuff,
Rub it with salt, it then goes well enough.
Thus, you perceive, all works have been at fault,
To doubt the potency of Richmond salt;
It sweetens and removes a doubtful flavor.
We once, indeed, had coffee, but we fear
Our friends have found the article too dear;
So now, we eat our sumptuous breakfast dry,
For, even they use coffee made from rye;
Some time we Yankees may the secret steal,
And make pure Java from bad Indian meal;
At all their little failings we must wink,
And so *ad libitum* foul water drink;
Such is our morning meal; now, "what's for dinner?"
Asks some insatiate half-starved sinner,
As if the bounty of our christian friends
Was not enough to answer nature's ends.
The fellow craves till problem number two
Calls the attention of a hungry crew
That in a corner squat in deep reflection,
Like cabinet ministers on home protection;
With busy hands, at length, their pates they scratch,
As if their brains a dinner there could hatch;
'Twould seem, they had with one consent resolved
To scratch until the problem had been solved.
Others, again, beguile the weary hours
With quiet game of cribbage, or all-fours;—
Wrapt in a cloud of smoke from morn till noon,
They don't expect a dinner from the moon.
The sick lie on the floor as mute as mice,
Poor *devils*, thankful for a little rice;
While lame and lazy, seeming ill at ease,
Are laying plans their hunger to appease.
Some fellows who are lucky, having money,
Though Yankees think the medium rather funny,
With bogus bills of small denominations,
Contrive to add a little to their rations;
And eat at noon without a guilty blush,
A pint of Indian meal, made into mush;
Another brings to view his precious store:
A bone, that he had picked too well before;
This, (our pants inform us we are thinner,)
Makes the sum total of our prison dinner.
I now shall place in order proper,
The dainty items of our prison supper:

At five o'clock, and sometimes half-past five,
A humming sound is heard throughout the hive;
The boarders think their supper rather late,
And beat the deil's tattoo upon their plates;
Some get impatient, and the rest they choke
In stifling clouds of vile tobacco smoke;
For, be it known, a hogshead found up stairs
Affords the boys a chance to "put on airs."
So those to whom the habit is quite new,
Can smoke a pipe, or take a lucious chew;
But as the boarders throng around the door,
Our colored gemman enters as before,
With graceful dignity, his load removes,
While some thin wretch his tardiness reproves.
Meanwhile, another of the sable race,
Whose comic grin o'erspreads his ebon face,
Upon his neighbor's heels had followed close,
And in his hands a curious looking dose,
But something floating meets the boarders' view,
It must be, yes it is, an Irish stew;
Just then the eyes of hungry sinners gleam,
Extended nostrils scent the fragrant stream,
The grinning darkey on his fingers blows,
His scalded hands to impatient boarders shows,
Then leaves his steaming buckets on the floor,
And with another grin he shuts the door.
Now, anxious to inspect the savory mess,
The hungry boarders round the buckets press,
But, short and tall, their open mouths they droop,
Their Irish stew is regulation soup:
Their happiness is changed to speechless grief,
The water, this, in which they boiled their beef;
Some friendly hand to make it somewhat thicker,
Had dropped a cracker in the tasteless liquor;
Of this, each boarder shares a standard gill,
Is quite enough, and warranted to kill.
To test its strength on us is their intention,
All the ingredients I dare not mention.
We crumble in our ounces, six, of bread,
Swallow the physic, and then go to bed;
This, be it known, is on hard boards,
The best the prison discipline affords;
Shades of the epicures of ancient Rome,
Whose deeds are writ in many an ancient tome,
Ye mighty men whose gastronomic feats
Were sung in ballads in Rome's ancient streets,
Whose wondrous deeds by Plato have been noted,
And crests by modern epicures been quoted,
Hold fast your laurels, for in Richmond Prison,
E'en at this day, your rivals have arisen;
Who, though they cannot boast a second course,
Have called from morn until their throats were hoarse;
Insatiate men, whose inwards nought can fill,
Not even tubs of stuff called wholesome swill;
Who crammed their stomachs with suspicious beef,
Would taint the fingers of a starving thief;

Whose hungry eyes, most starting from their sockets,
Proclaiming they are starving men, with empty pockets;
Who eat with gusto the Confederate swill
That would a famished jackal surely kill;
Assembled round Secession's filthy tub,
Hyena-like, their eyes devour their grub;
Nor can they have it in their hands too soon,
But bolt it, dog-like, without fork or spoon,—
Then, with a rag, moustaches must they wipe;
Such rare perfection in the mystic art
Might cause the souls of richer men to start.
The famous soger may safely bood it,
That he and all his tribe have got to hood it,
And open shops where science is unknown,
In some place bordering on the frigid zone.
And tell the epicure, he may find there
His fame was lost by this, our BILL OF FARE!

Some of the prison guards not unusually displayed their authority in the commission of the most gratuitous and unprovoked outrages. The notorious Lieut. Todd was singularly vicious and brutal in his treatment of the prisoners, and seldom entered the room without grossly insulting some of the inmates. He invariably appeared with a drawn sword in his hand, and his voice and manner, as he addressed the prisoners, always indicated a desire to commit some cruel wrong. Upon one occasion, with the flat edge of his weapon, he severely struck in the face an invalid soldier, who had not obeyed the order to fall-in for roll-call, with sufficient alacrity! At another time, one of the guard, in the presence and with the sanction of Todd, struck a prisoner upon the head with the butt-end of a musket. It is not to be wondered at that this ferocious and vindictive monster should be regarded with feelings of the deepest horror and detestation, and it was with the highest satisfaction that we learned he was to be superseded for his tyrannical conduct. What "benefits" we realized from a change of administration, will appear in the course of the narrative.

I believe that some of the prisoners attribute to Todd the crime of shooting some of our comrades; or, at least, believe that the shooting was done by his orders. To give the d—l his due, I must admit there was no satisfactory evidence of this; and conclude that such acts were voluntary upon the part of the sentinels. Whenever approaching the window, we were threateningly warned by the guard below, to stand back, etc.; but the curiosity of some of our poor fellows, hungering and thirsting for a glimpse of the outer world, sometimes overcame their apprehension of danger, and they suffered according.

The first victim of these Sepoy atrocities was private M. C. Beck, of the 79th Regiment. He was instantly killed by a musket ball, fired by one of the guard, while he (Beck) was in the act of hanging up his blanket, on the *inside* of the window, to dry. Shortly after this occurrence, private R. Gleason, of the N. Y. Fire Zouaves, was likewise shot while looking from the window. His murderer (the guard) is said to have remarked, as he leveled his musket, "See me take that d—d Zouave in the eye!" The ball entered his forehead, and he fell instantly dead.

Four men of our number were seriously wounded in this manner, and one, private C. W. Tibbetts, instantly killed, under circumstances which were peculiarly flagrant and indefensible. The prisoners were occasionally permitted to visit, in couples, an out-house in the prison yard, and as Tibbetts and a companion were going thither, *with the consent of the guard,* a sentinel on the opposite side deliberately raised his piece and fired at them. The ball passed through the breast of Tibbetts, killing him instantly, and wounding his companion in the arm.

These atrocities passed unnoticed by the Richmond press, save in a single instance, the case of private Gleason, which elicited from the Dispatch the following mysterious falsification:

"SUDDEN DEATH.—A Yankee prisoner named Gleason, a member of the Eleventh New York Regiment, died very suddenly yesterday at the Confederate States Prison No. 1; cause, concussion of the brain, brought on by violent expectoration."

The indignation of the prisoners at these skulking and cowardly assassinations, could find no adequate expression; yet as the bleeding forms of their murdered comrades were one after another borne from their presence to the "negro burying ground," they felt that a day of Retribution, however long deferred, would be found in the book of the future.

The successor of Todd was a Switzer named Wurtz, a vulgar, swaggering fellow,

"Full of strange oaths, and bearded like the pard,"

and immensely inflated with the dignity of his position. The odor of his presence led to the suspicion that he had but a limited appreciation of the water privileges outside, or else improved them in homeopathic doses. His jargon was excessively amusing, and whenever the prisoners affected to misunderstand, he was thrown into a spasmodic rage.

I have spoken of the inferior quality and quantity of our food, but under the administration of Wurtz, we sometimes got nothing but bread and water. The escapes from the prison were numerous. Not less than one hundred in all, succeeded in getting away, but I believe all but eight were recaptured. Whenever an escape was discovered, Wurtz entered the prison in a towering passion, and with a series of frantic gestures commanded the prisoners to fall in for roll-call. The fugitive, of course, did not respond. The keeper then demanded to know the circumstances attending his escape, but the prisoners refused to answer any of his queries. " Tell me," he said, " or you shall never be so sorry in your life. I shall keep you tree tays on pred and wasser."

" Oh, ho !" shouted a dozen voices, " Three cheers for Wurtz. He will keep us three days on bread and butter !"

" No, no, you tam villians. I say pred and wasser—*wasser*, not busser !"

And Wurtz was as good as his word.

CHAPTER VI.

At one extremity of the room on the second floor, was a small enclosure which had formerly been used as an office, and in which the proprietors of the manufactory had stored a quantity of tobacco, and a barrel of sweetened rum used for flavoring the same. The door of this mystic chamber had been nailed up, but sundry reconnoisances thereabout had established the fact above noted. A saw was accordingly manufactured from an old case-knife, and with this rough implement an entrance was effected and the contents of the room " confiscated" for the benefit of loyal citizens. I am confident that some of the prisoners appropriated a sufficient quantity of " Old Virginia Twist" to meet their necessities for many months; and as to the " sweetened rum," it is not to be wondered at that after such long abstinence, there should have been an excess of " rapture" at this unexpected—*discovery*.

Sergeant Wurts was not long in ascertaining that the " tam Yankees," as he invariably termed them, were in unusual " *spirits*," and upon detecting their burglary and depredations, he fell into a paroxysm of rage, and demanded the names of the ringleaders. His investigation was unsuccessful, and, as usual, he determined to punish all. In this instance the sentence was quite severe, " Three days on bread and water, and then to be sent to New Orleans." This threat was fulfilled to the letter. After the bread and water diet, 250 of our number, (there were about 300 in all in the first and second stories,) were shipped to the Crescent City. Their places were soon refilled from the general hospital, and by prisoners more recently taken in Western Virginia.

Sergeant Wurtz seemed not unconscious that these acts of petty tyranny might one day "return to plague the inventor," and upon one occasion he went below, to the officers' quarters, and unbosomed himself in the following fashion :

" Vat you tink dem Yankees do, if dey get *me* prisoner, up Nort—eh ? "

He was assured they would not hurt him, on any account.

"Oh!" said he, (I omit his profanity,) "I know besser. Dey will kill me sure! But I shall take care dey vill no catch me—but if dey do (shrugging his shoulders) I am certain dey will kill me so quick—so quick, I tell you—dat I shall know notting about it —ugh!"

And that was the only opinion ever expressed by the valorous Sergeant, in which the prisoners seemed heartily to concur.

The two hundred and fifty who were to be sent to New Orleans were composed of those who had not been wounded, together with such as had recovered from their injuries. Among these were private Conway, of Rochester, and Orderly Sergeant Joslyn, of Brockport, both of the 13th Regiment. Large crowds had assembled about the prison in anticipation of their departure, and as the prisoners were drawn up in line to be marched to the depot, every spectator must have been impressed by the fact that, notwithstanding their destitute condition—most of them being coatless, and many of them hatless and shoeless—they were a far superior class of men, both in point of physical vigor and intelligence, to the poor wretches who formed their escort. This fact was conceded even by Confederate officers, who seemed to regard their private soldiers generally, with a feeling of loathing and contempt. Why? Because, in a word, they were (as a class) the ignorant and degraded creatures known as the "poor whites of the South"—a people so contaminated by the moral filth of slavery as to have become the supple tools and implements of an unscrupulous oligarchy.

It was a gloomy day to all of us—yet less so than it would have been but for this refreshing contrast. The parting salute of our unfortunate comrades before evacuating the prison, was "three cheers for the Stars and Stripes," and the very walls and rafters of the old warehouse seemed to throb and quaver with the reverberations. A moment afterward they were marching below, and as they passed the prison windows, with the firm and elastic tread of veteran soldiers, every form was proudly erect, and many a beaming glance was cast backward to the prison windows, as happy voices shouted a last "Good-bye, Yankees! We're bound for Dixie!" They seemed every one determined that the enemy should have no occasion for exultation, and the citizens of Richmond must have looked with unaffected astonishment upon these manifestations of a loyal spirit, which no act of "Confederate" tyranny could either check or conquer.

I may mention that among the prisoners sent to New Orleans was Sergeant Steward, of the 14th Brooklyn. He was a Northerner by birth, (a citizen of Hopedale, Mass.,) but had lived in Richmond, where he was employed as an agent for the Sloat Sewing Machine Company, and during his residence there he had formed a matrimonial engagement with a young lady of genteel and respectable parentage. Upon the commencement of hostilities, however, he returned to the North, and enlisted under the old flag. He was captured at Bull Run and imprisoned, as above noticed. By some means his betrothed learned of his misfortune, and being unable to obtain admittance to the prison, she daily appeared on the opposite side of the street, walking to and fro, and communicating with her lover by signs, as he stood near the window.

On the day when the prisoners were sent away she was early at her post, and carried in her hands a small parcel which she evidently designed to present to him; but she was not permitted to approach or speak with him, and she joined the throng which followed the prisoners, weeping bitterly. Subsequently, we frequently saw her promenading in her accustomed place, opposite the prison, gazing wistfully at the window at which her lover was wont to appear, as though a melancholy consolation were to be derived from a picture ever present to her imagination. The prisoners were all affected by these mournful evidences of her womanly devotion, and the subject was seldom referred to except with expressions of the deepest sympathy for the unfortunate couple.

> "Had they never loved sae kindly,
> Had they never loved sae blindly,
> Never met nor never parted,
> They had ne'er been broken-hearted."

The name of the young lady is Sarah Swards. I should have withheld its publication, but for the fact that a brother of Sergeant Steward has written to me since my return, certifying to the truth of my original narrative of this occurrence, and giving the lady's name. This letter was inadvertently published, and hence there is no longer any occasion for the suppression of any of these facts.

Chaplain Mines, of the 2d Maine Regiment, was among the prisoners taken at Bull Run, and was an inmate of the officers' quarters. He was permitted to visit the second floor for a short time every Sabbath, for the purpose of conducting public worship,. and upon one occasion, in concluding the services, he gave out the National Hymn "America"—

> "My country, 'tis of thee,
> Sweet land of Liberty,
> Of thee I sing."

It was sung by all of the prisoners, and with great feeling. Hardly had the services concluded, when the patriotic Chaplain was

3

informed by the Confederate officers that they were not to be insulted by such demonstrations, and as a penalty for his misbehavior, he would not thereafter be allowed to pass from the officers' quarters to the second floor.

We were thus deprived for a long time of the Chaplain's kindly ministrations; but this proceeding, so far from suppressing the obnoxious demonstrations, rather tended to aggravate the same, for on the succeeding Sundays, afternoon, the boys sang not only "America," but the "Star Spangled Banner," and then concluded the "services" with three ringing cheers for the Stars and Stripes.

On one occasion Lieut. Emac, a West Point graduate, (one of the officers in charge of the post,) entered the room with his drawn sword, and demanded the name of the prisoner who "started the singing;" whereupon a young man instantly stepped out and modestly remarked that he *believed* he was the man. Emac was not a little disconcerted at this proceeding, and retorted by several insulting expressions, calling him a Yankee coward, etc.

To this the prisoner coolly responded that if Emac would lay down his weapons and "step out," he (the speaker,) would show him which was the best man of the two!

The Lieutenant answered by saying that "if it was not for the name of the thing—of striking an unarmed man, and a prisoner —he would cut him down."

This chivalric fellow was familiarly known as "Bowie Knife," an appellation derived from the fact that on a former occasion, he gravely asserted that he was in the battle of Bull Run, and there killed one Brigadier General, two commissioned officers and three privates—all with a bowie knife. He flattered himself that he was a terror to the Yankees, but the above anecdote aptly illustrates the estimation in which he was held by "unarmed prisoners."

CHAPTER VII.

The circumstances attending the capture of Chaplain Mines, an Episcopal minister (previously referred to), were somewhat peculiar. Upon entering the field he took his place in the ranks as a private soldier, and fought till the wounded and dying required his clerical attentions. He was taken prisoner while thus engaged, near Falls Church. His valise, containing his surplice, service books, family daguerreotypes and private wardrobe, was taken from him, and shortly after his removal to Richmond a "brother" clergyman paid him a visit of condolence in the prison, and had the effrontery to confess that the articles which Mr. Mines had lost, had been presented to him (the visitor), as *his share* of the trophies of the day.   Mr. Mines solicited, and of course expected, a restitution of this ecclesiastical plunder, but his reverend brother bluntly declined to disgorge, remarking, that as a prisoner Mr. M. should be treated with all due circumspection; and adding that if he (the Southern Chaplain) should meet with a similar misfortune, he hoped he would receive an equal degree of consideration at the hands of the Federals.

Mr. Mines replied that the Federal Government did not make war on Confederate Chaplains, and if by chance he (the visitor) should be taken prisoner, he would be released with a fitting apology for the act.   He further stated that if he was himself released before the termination of the war, he had determined to rejoin his regiment as a commissioned officer, and thenceforth make fighting the *rule* instead of the *exception*.   I am happy to state that he has been released, and is now, I trust, in a position which he is so well qualified to fill.

There was so little to relieve the monotony of prison life in the quarters of the private soldiers, that it was often a satisfaction to learn that our guard had devised some new annoyance as a penalty for wrong-doing.   Escapes, as I have before stated, were not unfrequent, and were generally effected in broad day.   The Confederate soldiers so often passed through the prison, that, with a change of guard, it was not difficult for a prisoner to counterfeit the dress and manner of a native, and pass the guard with impunity.   It needed only a suit of gray and a slouched hat, and sundry exchanges among the prisoners completed the rig.

Upon one occasion, while looking from the window to Hospital No. 2, which stood opposite our prison, I heard my name shouted, and glancing in the direction of the sound, I discovered my old comrade, Billy Hanlon.   He was lying upon a cot near a window, and was shaking at me, laughingly, the stump of his amputated leg.   I was so thrilled by the unexpected discovery, that without reflecting upon the probable consequences of the act, I brushed by the Confederate guard, passed through the prison yard, entered the hospital, and soon found my way to the cot of my crippled comrade.   After a short interview I returned in safety, and then learned that had not the guard supposed I was a Confederate soldier I would have been instantly *shot down* while passing from prison to hospital.

Eight of the prisoners escaped at one time, but they were all captured and brought back after a short interval.   It was customary to handcuff the returned fugitives, but this method of restricting their liberty was without the desired effect; for as soon as the janitor's back was turned, *the shackles were unlocked* by a key which some ingenious Yankee had manufactured from his beef-bone!

Nothing in the world of art or mechanism is considered beyond the "craft" of a Yankee who is in possession of a jack-knife and a bunch of shingles, but I doubt whether, in case we had obtained shingles instead of bones, as the chief part of our rations, they could have been used to a more ingenious, purpose. After the bones were well picked, their value was greatly enhanced, and they not unfrequently became "bones of contention" among the prisoners when the "stock" ran low. There were few indeed who did not soon acquire the art of manufacturing, with knife and file, articles of ornament or utility, such as finger-rings, crosses, shields, dice, tooth-picks, dominoes, shirt-studs, sleeve-buttons, eagles, forks, spoons, and darning needles! Hence, although very few of the prisoners were habitually profane, it was not unusual to find one darning his stockings, while another was d——ing his corns. The trinkets were in great demand by the Confederate officers, and afforded a considerable revenue to the more industrious. Many a poor fellow has earned a palatable ration by the disposal of some choice sample of his cunning handicraft; and as we were denied the solace of books, these innocent employments sufficed in a great measure to lessen the tedium of a protracted imprisonment.

The diversions of the prisoners sometimes took the form of theatrical representations. I was informed that among the inmates of Prison No. 2, (which like Hospital No. 2, was adjacent to our own,) there were several professional actors, who, with the assistance of innumerable "supes," managed to render their performances highly successful. The audience were of course upon a dead level, but the programme invariably required that "front seats" should be reserved for cripples. The drama of Rob Roy was on one occasion presented to an "overflowing house." The Confederate officers who had consented to patronize the drama, were admitted at the rate of fifty cents per head. Few deadheads could pass the doorkeeper. The first part of the exhibition, Rob Roy, was highly applauded; but the after-piece, in which the author had embodied a scene at Bull Run, had a very depressing effect. The scene referred to illustrated the capture of a "Live Yankee" by ten Confederate soldiers, armed to the teeth with sharp sticks, and bristling with pasteboard bowies. Unfortunately for the success of the representation, the author had maliciously introduced some passages reflecting upon the gallantry of the Confederates. The result may be imagined. Our Con-♣ federate "patrons"

Stood not upon the order of their going,   ut went at once,

and ever after refused to lend their encouragement to the revival of even the "legitimate drama."

CHAPTER VIII.

Shortly after my removal from the hospital to the prison, I was permitted through the agency of Messrs. Ely and Huson, to visit the officers' quarters during the day, but at night was required to return to the second floor. This peculiar privilege was allowed me till, at the request of the commissioned officers generally, my name was transferred to their own list, and I thenceforth became a permanent occupant of the lower room.

There were between sixty and seventy in this department of the prison, ranking from Colonel to Lieutenant—the only civilians being Messrs. Ely and Huson of Rochester, Mr. Flagler of Virginia, and Mr. Taylor of Ohio. The public generally are familiar with the circumstances attending the capture of Messrs. Ely and Huson of Rochester. Mr. Flagler resided in the neighborhood of Bull Run (i. e., the battlefield), and he was arrested for harboring Mr. Huson. He was a kindhearted, christian gentleman; but respecting his political opinions this deponent sayeth not, for obvious reasons.

'Mr. Taylor was a citizen of Ohio, but was a property-holder in Virginia, and went thither in July to look after his estates. With a view to combine pleasure with business, he unfortunately ran out to take an observation while the battle of Bull Run was progressing, and was seized by the Confederates as an "alien enemy." He is a staunch Unionist, and during his captivity made no effort to repress his loyal sentiments.

Among the more distinguished officers confined in the prison when I arrived, were Colonels Corcoran and De Villiers and Major Porter. Subsequently Colonels Lee and Cogswell, Major Revere, and some twenty Captains and Lieutenants were added to our number from Leesburg.

During the first two or three months of their imprisonment, the officers enjoyed few conveniences superior to those of the privates; but after receiving remittances from the North, a considerable improvement was effected in this regard. Tables were erected, cots and blankets procured, and knives and forks were added to the facilities for eating. They clubbed together in messes, and lived chiefly at their own expense. Privates were employed for the culinary work, and everything, with the exception of the meat (which was prepared in the yard), was cooked over the gas-burners. The prison was furnished with one cylinder coal-stove, which answered only for heating purposes.

Messrs. Ely, Corcoran and three other officers, messed together, and Mr. Huson with the "Highland mess," which was composed of officers of the 79th. My own grateful acknowledgements for a similar favor are due to Lieuts. Parke, Booth, Hart, Kittridge, and Hancock. The meals were regularly served, three times per day, and in general the food was palatable, and though including few luxuries, was quite expensive. The standard bill of fare consisted of beef-steak and bread, (which was furnished by the Confederacy,) coffee, adulterated with corn, at $1,25 per pound; sweet potatoes, $1,50 per bushel. Our sugar cost 50c. per pound. Some of the messes obtained butter, which (if I remember correctly) cost seventy-five or eighty cents per pound; hams 25 and 30 cents. Eggs were scarce at 5 cents apiece; nutmegs, for an occasional pudding, ten cents each; whisky, on physician's "prescription," fifty cents a pint; common molasses, twenty-five cents per quart.

There was a great scarcity of provisions in Richmond, and "Lincoln's blockade" was denounced by the rebels in unmeasured terms. Salt sold from $18 to $26 per sack; boots, from $20 to $26 per pair; shoes, $7 to $15 ditto; clothing was fabulously high, and very little to be obtained at any price. Confederate uniform coats sold at $50 each; and complete suits were regarded cheap at $100. In the way of trimmings, yellow braid was substituted for gold lace, as there was none of the latter in market. Ordinary note paper cost two cents per sheet, and buff envelopes ditto. In short, ruinous prices were demanded for everything but cotton, and that was disgustingly plenty!

The origin of the Richmond Prison Association was a meeting of the officers to devise plans for their mutual comfort. It resulted in the election of a President and Secretary and the organization of a society under the above title, whose regular meetings were held weekly. Hon. Alfred Ely was the presiding officer, and Mr. Edwin Taylor the Secretary. The first order of business was the election of candidates, who were formally introduced in a speech from the "page," (Lieut. Hart,) and were afterwards requested to respond, which they usually did by recounting the manner of their capture, etc. The "test question" was then put—"What did you come down here for?" and then the fun commenced in earnest.

The following song, composed by the "page," (Lieut. Hart,) was sung in the prison every evening, to the tune of "Poor Pilgrim:"

Come, fellow prisoners, let's join in song;
Our stay in this prison, it won't be long.
CHORUS—Roll on, roll on, sweet moments roll on,
And let the poor prisoner go home, go home.

Our friends at home have made a demand,
To have returned this patriot band.
     (Chorus and repeat.)

The public press they are bound to obey,
For from the people they receive their pay.
     (Chorus and repeat.)

Congressman Ely is first on the list;
He'll soon be there, our friends to assist.
     (Chorus and repeat.)

And give to his mind its widest range,
To "spread himself" on the theme of exchange.
     (Chorus and repeat.)

This is the way I long have sought,
And mourned because I found it not.
     (Chorus and repeat.)

If you get there before I do,
Look out for me, for I'm coming too.
     (Chorus and repeat.)

For now that the thing has got a start,
They have concluded to send old Hart.
     Roll on, roll on, sweet moments roll on,
     And let the poor prisoner go home, go home.

The enchanting effect with which this mellifluous and affecting production was rendered by the united voices of the Association, usually attracted a large crowd of citizens to the prison windows; and it was the general conviction of the inmates that the nation had lost a brilliant poet in winning a gallant soldier.

The sessions of the society were highly entertaining and its records are worthy of preservation. Mr. Ely, I understand, has in his possession a report of the proceedings taken by himself, including sketches of the speeches, &c., which he proposes soon to publish, in connection with his own experiences of prison life.

I need not dwell upon the incidents of our prison life, many of which, however, I think would bear repetition. I shall relate but a single one in this connection, as an illustration of the proverb that truth is stranger than fiction.

I have before stated that some of the private soldiers, from the upper rooms, were employed in the officers' quarters, a service which they gladly accepted as affording superior rations. Among these was Corporal M——n of New York, a young man of wealthy parentage, of attractive manners, good intellectual endowments, and withal "handsome as Apollo."

At the request of some of the officers he was occasionally permitted to visit the lower floor, and upon one occasion was allowed to leave the prison on parole, for the purpose of purchasing supplies. While thus passing through one of the main thoroughfares, M———n was accosted by a little girl, who presented him with a boquet, at the same time pointing to a young lady on the opposite side of the street, as the donor. The Corporal acknowledged the gift by a polite bow, and proceeded upon his mission: The lady, apparently fascinated, followed him at a distance, to the prison, and as he entered it, reciprocated his salute, and leisurely walked away.

For some inexplicable cause the Corporal was not again permitted to go out, and a negro,—I should have mentioned that quite a number (officers' servants) were in the prison—was despatched in his stead. The negro had not proceeded far, when he was met by the young lady referred to, and the sequel to their interview was developed in a package with which he returned to the officers' quarters, and delivered to Corporal M———n. It was found on examination to contain a *new suit of clothes*, and upon one garment was pinned a small card, neatly inscribed with the name of his benefactress—

"Only this, and nothing more."

Corporal M———n instantly addressed himself to the task of epistolary composition, in which he gracefully acknowledged the receipt of the gift, and expressed his heartfelt thanks. This was delivered by the negro on the day following, and he returned with a package containing a number of pocket-handkerchiefs, socks and shirts!

As in the first instance, the only communication which accompanied the gift was the donor's card. The Corporal again acknowledged his obligations by a polite note, which was duly delivered through the same medium.

Thenceforth the Corporal was in daily receipt of the choicest dainties, and a regular epistolatory correspondence was carried on until the day of his release, which occurred on the 3d of January. A matrimonial engagement had been made during the interval, with the understanding that the parties would meet in Baltimore on the 1st of March next.

I have omitted to state that the Corporal had been sent back to his old quarters, but having ascertained that his fair *inamorata* daily promenaded within view of the officers' quarters, he obtained employment below as cook, and was thereafter unfailingly at his post to reciprocate the loving smiles of his betrothed.

She had sent him her daguerreotype, which he frequently exhibited to me. It was a lovely image, and one that would have required no "collateral" inducement to carry captive the most frigid or lethargic fancy. I learned that she was of a wealthy family, and of as "good blood" as was to be found among the F. F. V.'s, and her letters, I was assured, evinced that she was no less intelligent than refined.

When the glad tidings of our release came, the name of Corporal M———n was found in the list. This intelligence was quickly conveyed to his yearning admirer, and he expected once more to see or communicate with her before leaving Richmond. We saw nothing of her, however, as we marched through the streets of Richmond, though the Corporal's longing vision was strained at every animate object.

But when a halt was ordered, a fine carriage, driven by a negro, suddenly made its appearance, and stopped at a short distance from our ranks. A lady descended—there was a brief, but earnest colloquy among the Confederate officers of our guard—and the next moment the enraptured twain (Corporal M———n and his romantic affianced) stood face to face! A few words, the first they had ever exchanged in person, were hurriedly spoken, in subdued, yet melting tones; the engagement was sacredly renewed—their faces were for a moment lighted, as with a flame—there was a fervent, thrilling pressure of their hands, and they separated!

A circumstance is connected with the daguerreotype, above referred to, which deserves a passing notice. Before it left the prison, the picture was taken from the case, and a small slip of paper, closely written, and addressed to Gen. McClellan, was deposited therein, and the daguerreotype then replaced. On reaching Washington the paper was safely delivered to the commander-in-chief, a meeting of the Cabinet was called, and the day following *there was a leak stopped*—a mysterious leak, from high official circles, and which had inestimably benefited the rebels for many months.

CHAPTER IX.

The question of "exchange" was naturally uppermost in the mind of every prisoner, and was at intervals an untiring theme of discussion. One had but to lisp the word, and a crowd of his associates was instantly gathered about him, canvassing the subject with as much interest and energy as though it were newly broached, and extracting fresh encouragement from every sage or emphatic observation predicting a speedy release.

It was our first impression that we would be detained but for a few days; that the Federal Government only needed to be apprised of our situation, and our numbers, to proffer the requisite exchanges from the prisoners in its own custody. This opinion at length yielded to the belief that another advance was contemplated, and that our own destiny depended, in a great measure,

upon the result of a second battle.   A new apprehension here
presented itself, for it was openly threatened by the rebels that,
in the event of their defeat at *Manassas*, the Union prisoners
would be assassinated by the Confederate soldiers in Richmond!
I confess that I had less fear of the Richmondites than of a
reckless, infuriated and *retreating* army.

It will be borne in mind that certain of the Richmond press
were particularly hostile to the prisoners.   When it was rumored
that Colonel Brown of Fort Pickens meditated an attack upon the
navy-yard at Pensacola, several of the more influential of the
Southern journals earnestly advocated the policy of filling the
navy-yard with Union prisoners; arguing that Brown would then
be compelled either to sacrifice his own friends or to altogether
withhold an attack.

But harrassed by such reports, we still remained in Richmond,
and as the weary days and weeks were added to our confinement,
without affording the slightest prospect of a release, the most
hopeful became disheartened.   The official indifference manifested at Washington toward us seemed unaccountable.   We
could not understand why the Government was unwilling even to
meliorate the condition of men who had fought honorably in its
defence, and had thus not only become *prisoners*, but were known
to be actually suffering from the want of food and clothing.   Yet
notwithstanding these discouragements, I believe that at no period
would any member of the Richmond Prison Association have
consented to receive his discharge at the sacrifice of a single prin-
ciple involving the national honor.   And these reflections lead me
to the narration of the most painful chapter of my prison experi-
ence—viz: the illness and death of Calvin Huson, Jr.

Mr. Huson was at the time of his capture in feeble health.
The fatigues of the day had so nearly exhausted his physical
powers that he was obliged to seek temporary rest and shelter at
the farm house of Mr. Flagler, near Centerville.   Had he been
aware, as he afterward informed me, that it was a place of danger,
he would have pushed forward at any cost, and could have easily
effected his escape.   He was taken prisoner on the morning of
Tuesday, the 23d of July, the second day following the battle,
and was instantly conveyed to Manassas, and after a few days de-
tention, to Richmond, where he was placed in Prison No. 1.
When I first saw him, seven weeks after his capture, he had very
perceptibly changed.   He had lost that healthful glow of countenance and the "judicial plumpness" of figure, which I had formerly observed, and his habitual expression was one of settled
melancholy.   It was plain to perceive that he was suffering from
serious ill health, and though endeavoring to appear easy, pleasant

and unconcerned, in his social intercourse, this was evidently accomplished with much effort. .

During my first conversation with him, he adverted. with a feeling of deep anxiety to the probable distress of his family at his unexpected misfortune, and to the unsettled state of his private business affairs. He looked forward to his examination, however, with the utmost confidence, feeling satisfied that he would not be unduly detained by the rebel government a moment after he had been afforded a hearing. But in this he was sadly mistaken, and it was, perhaps, owing to the unchangeable conviction of his mind that he was soon to receive his discharge, that he was so overwhelmed by the announcement to the contrary.

His examination took place before C. S. Commissioner at Richmond on the 18th of September, as I find by reference to my Diary. He was then quite ill, though not confined to his bed. The decision of the Commissioner, which was for several days withheld, was announced to Mr. Huson by Gen. Winder, and was briefly to the effect that he would be held as a prisoner of war. Though this was a severe blow to Mr. Huson, he bore it with unaffected dignity and resignation.

About the 28th of September his health began rapidly to decline, and from that time forward he was constantly confined to his bed. His disease was pronounced to be typhoid fever. Dr. E. G. Higginbotham was his physician, and was unremitting in professional attentions, but evidently—and as Mr. Huson himself assured me—"the Doctor did not understand his case." All in the officers' quarters deeply sympathised with him, and would have made any sacrifice in their power for his restoration.

Mr. Ely was likewise kindly attentive, and subsequently obtained his removal to the residence of Mrs. John Van Lew. Had this transfer been effected at an earlier date, the unfortunate man would have been spared much needless suffering. The incessant noise and confusion upon the second floor was a source of constant disquiet to the patient, and rendered it impossible for him to sleep; yet Mr. Ely's request for his removal was disregarded until within five days of his death.

Prior to this I was frequently at the bedside of the sufferer, and watched with him three consecutive nights. He conversed a great deal, and to that end expressed a wish that he might constantly have a companion, saying that he wanted "to talk to some one, or to have some one talk to him." His mind usually reverted to his home, and often dwelt upon topics of public interest in Rochester. In reviewing his own official career as District Attorney, he adverted freely to the more important trials—the Ira Stout case, etc. Alluding to another important trial, and one which created a remarkable sensation at the time, he spoke of it as the most

earnestly contested case in which he ever participated, and confessed to the deep mortification he had experienced at his defeat.
He said that his convictions of the guilt of the party had under-
gone no change.

Another significant remark may with propriety be quoted here.
Respecting the hardships of close confinement to one who had formerly enjoyed the most perfect freedom and active habits of life,
he felt that in his position as District Attorney he had not appre-
ciated the feelings of the criminals whom he had convicted, when
arraigned to receive their sentences ; and he felt that were he ever
again to occupy the position of prosecuting attorney—though, if
convinced of the guilt of the accused, it would be his duty to labor
for his conviction—he would nevertheless recommend him to the
mercy of the court.   It was his consolation to know that he had
never striven to convict a prisoner whom he believed to be innocent of the charge.   On the other hand, he assured me, that in
cases of this character, where he had become fully convinced of
the guiltlessness of the accused, he had adjourned the case, con-
sulted with the defendant's attorney, and given him the advanta-
ges of his own discoveries.

Mr. Huson early confessed to an apprehension that he would
not recover.   He said there was something in the atmosphere of
Rebeldom that poisoned his whole being.   At a later period, and
when quite low, he expressed the opinion that if he could but once
more reach his home, or even once more stand under the flag of
the United States, he would become a well man.   Mr. Huson
conversed much upon the subject of religion, and I believe that he
died in the Christian faith.   I frequently approached his couch,
under the supposition that he was asleep, and found him to be
engaged in earnest and heartfelt prayer.   During the latter part
of his illness his mind frequently wandered, and he expressed to
me a fear that should he recover his health, his mental faculties
would remain impaired.   In his lucid intervals he was always
tranquil, for he had fortified himself against the worst event, and
seemed only to grieve for his family.   And thus by degrees—

> "He faded, and so calm, so meek,
> So softly worn, so sweetly weak,
> So tearless, yet so tender, kind,
> And grieved for those he left behind.
>
> *   *   *   *   *   *   *
>
> "A little talk of better days,
> A little, *our own* hopes to raise ;
> Yet not a word of murmur, not
> A groan o'er *his* untimely lot."

I cannot forbear mentioning here, to the everlasting disgrace
and infamy of Capt. Gibbs, the (Confederate) officer of the post,

that on the day of Mr. Huson's removal to the house of Mrs.
Van Lew, he was required to *sign a parol of honor* not to attempt
an escape. Though suffering from extreme exhaustion, unable to
sit up in bed, and regarded by all his fellow prisoners as a dying
man, he was yet compelled by the rebel officer to execute this
parol. In order to do this, two of his fellow prisoners assisted to
raise him up, and the paper was duly subscribed. It was happily
the last "duty" which Mr. Huson was required to perform.

The sufferer was very kindly cared for in the family of Mrs.
Van Lew, and Dr. Higginbotham was, as usual, faithful and untiring in his professional attentions. But deprived of the society
of his familiar friends, and practically cut off from the sympathies
which had buoyed him up during his prison confinement, the
sufferer rapidly declined; and on the morning of the 14th of October, Mr. Ely received a brief note from Mrs. Van Lew, announ-
cing that his friend was at the point of death. Mr. Ely repaired
as speedily as possible to the house, but before his arrival Mr.
Huson had expired.

The funeral was attended from the house of Mrs. Van Lew, by
the Rev. Dr. Mines, officiating clergyman, and Mr. Ely. The re-
mains had, by order of Mr. Ely, been placed in a metallic burial
case, and were interred in the Protestant Cemetery, near the General Hospital.

The only letter addressed to Mr. Huson, which ever reached
Richmond, was delivered to Mr. Ely on the day following Mr.
Huson's decease.

Soon after his death, a special meeting of the Prison Association was held, and suitable notice taken of the event. Addresses
were made by Messrs. Ely, Flagler of Va., Mines of Maine, Church
of Rhode Island, Taylor of Ohio, and others. The Masonic Fraternity, of which Mr. Huson was a member, was represented in
the persons of several prisoners. I present the resolutions which
they adopted:

F. A. M.

Whereas, The members of the fraternity of Free and Accepted Ma-
sons, who are prisoners of war in the city of Richmond, Virginia, have
heard with deep regret of the death of Calvin Huson, Jr., Esq., a Royal
Arch Mason of distinguished standing in the city of Rochester, N. Y.,
and late our fellow prisoner: Therefore,

Resolved, That we convey to the wife and family of the deceased, our
sincere sympathy in their bereavement: feeling that, as they have lost
the devoted husband and father, so we mourn one who was an able man,
a warm-hearted brother, and an ornament to our Order.

Resolved, That it is our duty to send our testimony to the brethren
who were connected with the Lodge and Chapter of our deceased brother, as to our appreciation of his noble qualities of head and heart.

Resolved, That the Rev. Bro. Mines be requested to transmit these
resolutions to the family of the deceased, and to our brethren at home

with the request that they be published, as a testimony on our part of
the high esteem in which brother Huson was held.

Comp. JOHN F. MINES, } Chairman.
Grand Chaplain of G. L. of Maine, }

Comp. M. A. PARKE, Excelsior Chapter No. 12, Michigan, Sec'y.
RICHMOND, Va., Oct. 19th, 1861.

The Brethren F. A. M. convened on the 19th of October, were the
following, viz:

Comp. Rev. John F. Mines, Chaplain 2d Maine.
"   Lieut. M. A. Parke, 1st Michigan.
"   Capt. William Manson, 79th N. Y. S. M.
"   Lieut. Thomas B. Glover, 4th Maine.
Broth. Lieut. Robert Campbell, 79th N. Y. S. M.
"   Samuel Irwin, 2d N. Y. S. M.
"   Assistant Sergeant William B. Fletcher, 6th Indiana.
RICHMOND, Nov. 5th, 1861.

The loss of Mr. Huson was unfeignedly mourned by all of the
prisoners, for as a community in misfortune they had fitly appre-
ciated the companionship of one whose high personal worth com-
mended him to the sincere affection of every member.

> "Eternal spirit of the chainless mind,
> Brightest in prison, LIBERTY, thou art!
> For there thy habitation is the *heart*—
> The heart, which love of thee alone can bind;
> And when thy sons to prisons are consigned,
> *   *   *   *   *   *   *   *   *
> Their country conquers with their martyrdom,
> And Freedom's fame finds wings on every wind!"

CHAPTER X.

No menagerie was ever regarded with more general interest
and curiosity in a country village, than were the Union prisoners
in the tobacco warehouses of Richmond. They were the standard
attraction of people of both sexes, all ages, and every variety of
shade. On Sundays, more especially, the citizens turned out in
squads, and from morning till night, the street was blockaded
with eager spectators. The windows of our prison were low,
and though grated, a fair glimpse could be obtained of the inmates
without tip-toe exertion.

The prevailing expression of the crowd was one of intense
satisfaction, but there was an occasional glance of sympathy from
some of their number that secretly spoke volumes in our behalf.

Some of the Union officers would insist upon "stirring up the
animals," that we might "make sport for the Philistines." Mr. Ely
was designated as the "elephant," but as he had *lost his trunk at
Bull Run*, he had no disposition to appear on exhibition before the
deriding savages, notwithstanding frequent bids among the chiv-

alric gentry: "Where's the Little Man with the Big Head? I reckon I'd like to see him, and I'll give you ten dollars if you'll show him up!" The prison exchequer was low, but Mr. Ely entertained too mild an appreciation of Confederate currency to yield to the temptations which beset him.

One of the Union officers who had a taste for penciling, favored us with an illustration of the scene attending Mr. Ely's capture, as described by himself. The unfortunate M. C. appeared in the foreground, surrounded by numerous "masked batteries," which were belching all manner of leaden and fiery missiles, and to his evident discomfiture and alarm. In the background of the picture appeared the form of a "solitary horseman," bristling with wrath and bowies, and holding in one hand a monstrous revolver. He was in the act of demanding from the Congressman a surrender of his freedom or his life, and as discretion is the better part of valor, Mr. Ely diligently complied.

Mr. Ely received many visitors of distinction, including the redoubted Wigfall, Porcher Miles, Marshall and Breckinridge of Kentucky, Bishop Doane of South Carolina, and the celebrated Paul Morphy of New Orleans. The visit of the chess champion of the world might have been susceptible of an ironical interpretation, in view of our splendid opportunities at the prison window cross-bars. Mr. Breckinridge, I believe, expressed much sympathy for Mr. Ely, and engaged to use his best influence for his release.

About the time Mason and Slidell were captured, Mr. Ely became quite uneasy. It was understood a member of the Federal Congress proposed to confine these distinguished conspirators in dungeons, as hostages for Colonel Corcoran and others, and Mr. Ely naturally feared that in case this was done he would himself be compelled to accept of a similar compliment to his personal distinction. He accordingly dispatched Confederate Commissary Warner to "President" Davis, with a request to ascertain what he (Mr. Davis) thought his (Mr. Ely's) "chances" were. The Commissary fulfilled his mission, and returned with his tidings. He was met by Mr. Ely with a spring of joyful anticipation.

"Well." said the messenger. "I called upon the President as you requested and asked him what he thought your chances were."

"Yes—yes!" exclaimed the M. C., impatiently, "and what did Mr. Davis reply?"

"Why—why—his reply was, 'Well, Mr. Commissary, do you mean in this world or the next?'"

Mr. Ely winced slightly under a retort so uncourteous and so unexpected, but soon recovered his equanimity under the reflection, probably, that he might one day reciprocate the bogus President's politeness, either "in this world or the next"—provided, of course, that *Jeff.* should in due season arrive at the stool of *repentance.*

A pleasant episode one day occurred pending an interesting discussion among the prisoners on the subject of exchange. Mr. Ely was citing some unquestioned authority in relation to "what constitutes a belligerent?" when he suddenly espied among his outside listeners the dilapidated visage of a depreciated darkey, peering in at the windows. The speaker instantly dismissed the case in hand, and proceeded to "knock down" the chattel to the highest bidder. The purchaser, I believe, was Lieutenant Hart, at the round sum of $1,400. I seriously doubt whether the negro would have brought fourteen cents upon any block outside of the prison jurisdiction, a fitting commentary upon the financial ability and tact of a Northern member of Congress, who had been exposed but a few weeks to the slavery and secession virus.

There were many Southerners who cherished a vindictive hatred of the Federal Congressman and would, had they possessed the power, have sacrificed his life as unhesitatingly as they secured his person. In illustration of this fact I may state that on one occasion he very narrowly escaped the penalty at which I have hinted, and which would have settled the question of "exchange," so far as he was personally concerned, beyond controversy.

The circumstances of the affair may be briefly stated. Dr. Higginbotham had called upon Mr. Ely with the request that he would visit a wounded prisoner in the adjacent hospital. The patient had expressed a wish to see him, and Mr. Ely accordingly complied. As they left the officers' quarters, and were proceeding quietly in the direction of the hospital, they were observed by a Southerner of the class to which I have referred. As he recognized the Congressman, he exclaimed, "There goes that ——— abolitionist, Ely! I'll kill him, by ——!" and drawing a revolver he started on a rapid walk in pursuit. Fortunately for Mr. Ely, however, the threat of the fire-eater had been overheard by Capt. Gibbs, the rebel officer of the post, and he sprang after and overtook the would-be assassin before he had reached the other party. He immediately placed him under arrest, and led him away. Mr. Ely was happily unconscious of the peril in which he had been placed, and did not learn of it until three days afterward.

I have previously remarked that escapes from the prison were frequent, but the fugitives were almost invariably captured and brought back and subsequently sent further south.

In view, therefore, of the uncertainties attending this proceeding, many hesitated to attempt it, but in one instance a plan of escape was devised, which had it been carried out, I think would have resulted successfully. Mr. Ely had offered to pay the sum of $5,000 to any one who would "put him through" in safety, and this proposition had been accepted by Dr. Griswold. The latter enjoyed a standing parol, and was not long in searching out the right man for the undertaking. The person thus selected was an experienced engineer, who had been for many years employed on the James River and knew its every crook and inlet, and every forest upon its banks. It was determined to adopt this route, and it was thought that the voyage could be so timed that the party would travel only during the night and by day could find safe refuge in the forests. A suitable boat was accordingly procured, ample provisions were laid in store, the oars were muffled and all things were in readiness for the expedition, which was to start on the night following the completion of these arrangements. The party was to consist of four, but on the day preceding the night on which they were to leave the prison, Dr. Griswold was arrested and sent to New Orleans, where he soon after died, and the project was abandoned.

CHAPTER XI.

Many requests have been made to me that I should give some description of the *personnel*, discipline and general character of the rebel forces, so far as they came under my observation. My opportunities for such inspection were exceedingly limited, but I found occasion for the following impressions.

Regiments of Confederate soldiers frequently marched by the prison, destined for the field, and others were encamped about the city. The flower of the Southern army appeared to be in their cavalry forces, who were generally fine looking men, well mounted, graceful and spirited riders, and exceedingly well equipped. I was informed that they were chiefly representatives of the more wealthy families of the South. They were severally armed with carbine, revolvers, bowie-knife and saber.

The infantry, as a class, appeared to be less refined—in short, ignorant, unmannerly and brutal. Their prevailing physical characteristics indicated superior stature, sallowness of complexion, wiriness of frame, and a striking tendency to stoop-shoulders. They were poorly clad, and seemed to have an astonishing disregard of personal cleanliness. I seldom noticed any two members of a single company who were dressed alike. This was often a subject of remark among the Union prisoners, some of whom facetiously offered a standing premium for a discovery to the contrary. We had frequent opportunities of measuring their proficiency in drill and general tactics as compared with that of our own soldiers. Few seemed to understand their company

4

positions; the manœuvering was generally awkward in the extreme, and they marched with a slouching swagger which afforded lively recollections of a "general training" in the rural districts of New York.

Their habits indicated excessive indolence, and a love of tobacco and whisky that was all absorbing. Their arms in general consisted of the old U. S. flint lock musket, ("Floyd pattern,") and double-barreled shot-guns. In fact, all sorts of blunderbusses seemed to have been called into requisition.

While thus presenting facts derived from my own observation, I do not by any means assume that they are characteristic of the entire Southern army, but I think most of my comrades will bear me out in the assertion that some of the "military parades" which we witnessed in the rebel capital, quite partook of the nature of a *raree show*, the component parts of which were burlesque "Fusileers" and fantastic "Bologna Guards."

The demeanor of the rebel soldiers towards the prisoners, as they marched by our quarters, was often insulting in the extreme. We were frequently attracted to the windows by such shouts as "Good bye, Yankees; we'll soon send you more company!" etc. There were occasional retorts from the prisoners, and some observations respecting the possibility of their own (the rebels') defeat and capture, and these remarks, in turn, never failed to elicit from the enemy an eruption of slang, and specimen oaths. Indeed, the habit of profane swearing seemed positively indigenous to the "sacred soil," and was an intellectual pastime to which few of the natives were not addicted beyond the hope of reclamation. The unexpected sight of a live Yankee, was often provocative of the most wicked blasphemy imaginable.

Sickness prevailed in the Southern army to an alarming extent, and I was credibly informed that almost every unoccupied building in Richmond had been converted into a hospital, and filled with invalid soldiers from Manassas.

To such a strait was the "Confederacy" reduced for prison accommodations for even their own men, (held to answer charges of insubordination, etc.,) that they were frequently confined in the Union officers' quarters. Col. Adler of the "Wise Legion" was there for a time, an inmate of Prison No. 1. He had been arrested upon a charge of refusing to execute an order for retreat from the erratic and "invincible" Wise, and had been sentenced by the irascible General to be shot. The Colonel attempted to avoid the disgraceful penalty by cutting his own throat with his sword. The wound did not prove fatal, and he was conveyed to Prison No. 1. His case excited the sympathy of the Union officers, who felt that he was a better officer and a better man than Wise, and was indeed

"The noblest Roman of them all;"

and accordingly the officers treated him with much courtesy and consideration. But these fraternal manifestations were exceedingly ill-timed. The intimacy being observed by the Confederate authorities, Col. Adler was removed to the Richmond jail, probably on account of a suspicion that he might divulge something of importance to the "enemy." The Union officers were thus deprived of a clever associate, and one who eventually might have become a hopeful convert.

Among the "alien enemies" who were sent to the officers' quarters was an elderly Quaker, familiarly known as Father Pancost. He was a Virginian, and one of the few residing in the infected districts, who had had the hardihood to freely express his loyal sentiments in the midst of almost universal defection. The charge upon which he was arrested was of rather a novel character. He was the owner of a pet pigeon, which upon one occasion he was detected in conveying from his barn to his house. The "Confederate" inference was that it was no other than a *carrier pigeon*, which was regularly employed in transmitting treasonable messages to Washington! Hence the arrest and incarceration of Mr. Pancost. What became of his pigeon I am unable to state.

Father Pancost was a good natured, amiable gentleman, whose "thees" and "thous" imparted a pleasant charm to his conversation and rendered him at all times an agreeable companion. Among his many sterling virtues he possessed but a single weakness, but it was a weakness in which there was strength, and under the circumstances, quite excusable. Approaching me one day, shortly after his arrival, he inquired—"Friend, does thee know whether I can obtain any whisky from the keepers of this prison?"

I informed him that if he was ill, and could procure a whisky-prescription from one of the surgeons, it was not unlikely that he could obtain the liquor.

"But does thee think, friend, that I can obtain two quarts of whisky?"

I considered it rather doubtful, on the strength of a single prescription, but suggested that if he was frequently sick and could obtain as frequent prescriptions, he might in due course of time procure *quantum suff.*

This ended our conversation. The day following I discovered Father Pancost standing at the head of his cot—or in the place where his cot ought to be, for in truth he had none—and elevating to his lips a quart bottle. After an apparently generous

potation he replaced it in his satchel, which hung against the
wall, and walked away. It is perhaps due to myself to say that
this proceeding was observed by other prisoners, and as soon as
the old gentleman had gone to another part of the room some
person or persons to Father Pancost unknown, slyly abstracted
the bottle, clandestinely extracted its contents, refilled it with
water, and returned it to its original place.

In the course of his promenade, Father Pancost encountered
Mr. Ely, and after a brief interchange of sentiment, informed
him of his acquisition, and invited the M. C. to test its qualities—an
invitation which the latter did not. consider it expedient to decline. The bottle was once more taken from the satchel, and Mr.
Ely proceeded to uncork, the Quaker meantime expatiating
upon the superior merit of the distillation. The luxury of glasses
being quite unknown, the Congressman inverted the bottle in
primitive style, and for some time held it to his lips, staring at his
companion with an expression of mingled resentment and surprise, as being puzzled to determine whether he was the victim of
an accident or a "sell." The scene was decidedly comic, and
Mr. Ely was brought to a realizing sense of his predicament by
the smothered cachinnations of the lookers-on. Recovering his
self-possession, and smacking his lips with apparent relish, he
politely resigned the bottle and expeditiously retired.

Father Pancost was not insensible to the singularity of this
behavior, but it was fully explained as soon as he made a requisition upon his own account. Glancing around the room and
assuring himself that he was unobserved, he gravely (not to say
soberly) replaced the bottle in his satchel, and rejoined his associates with an expression of perfect unconcern.

The sequel to this amusing occurrence was reserved for the
evening. The fellow lodger of Father Pancost, or rather the
prisoner who slept nearest him, was Lieut. Hooper, of Philadelphia, a gentleman who had maintained the character of being an
uncompromising *Teetotaller*. He had scarcely retired for the night
when he was confronted by the stern and reproachful visage of
the defrauded Quaker, who with perfect deliberation and in the
severest accents delivered himself of the following homily.

"Friend, if thee took my bottle from my satchel and then
drank my whisky, thee didst very bad; but if thee drank the
whisky and then filled the bottle with water, thee didst very ——
d—d—decidedly bad!"

And Father Pancost turned away without waiting for any response.

"D—— him!" said Hooper, the next morning, "he *knows*
that I never drink!"

A less pleasant and acceptable companion than either Colonel Adler or Father Gleason was forced upon us by the Confederates in the person of Lieutenant Charles Van Gilson, a deserter from the Sickles Brigade. He had voluntarily entered the lines of the rebel army, and given himself up with the declaration that he would no longer fight for the Yankees, and had come over, to tender his services to the Confederate Government. The military authorities distrusted these assertions, and suspecting that he was a spy, sent him to Richmond for temporary confinement, and he was placed in the officers' quarters, in Prison No. 1. Supposing himself to be in the presence of Confederate officers, he repeated in substance his former declarations. The effect of this disclosure must have been anything but a pleasant surprise to the renegade. So highly exasperated were the officers, upon hearing his story, that he was immediately surrounded and seized—and a rope called for. I have no doubt whatever that if a rope could have been conveniently procured, the deserter would have as speedily met the fate he so richly merited. He however called loudly upon the guard, who entered and took him away. He was then sent to a prison occupied by private soldiers. By some chance they had been informed of the character of their uninvited guest, and scarcely five minutes had elapsed from the time of his entry, when he was assaulted by some of the prisoners, who bruised and kicked him, and were engaged in dragging him about the floor when he was again rescued by the guard. Of this fact I was assured by a Confederate officer. Van Gilson afterwards received a commission in the rebel army, and was sent to Kentucky. I read a notice of his promotion in the Richmond Dispatch.

CHAPTER XII.

The Richmond papers frequently boasted of accessions to their army from the Union prisoners. To what extent these declarations were true, I am unable to say; but the following list was prepared by a Union prisoner, who was for a time employed upon the prison records in Richmond:

William Clark, private, Company K, Third New Jersey Volunteers.

William Roach, private, Company D, Second Artillery, United States Army.

Michael Kelly, private, Company D, Second Artillery, United States Army.

Charles Tracy, Corporal, Company G, First Regiment, Sickles' Brigade.

Charles Van Gilson, Second Lieutenant, First Regiment, Sickles' Brigade.

W. Sherry, private, Company B, Twenty-sixth New York Volunteers.

L. Briggs, private, Company B, Twenty-sixth New York Volunteers.

J. A. Tompkins, Second United States Cavalry.

T. B. Remington, Thirtieth New York Volunteers.

Ernest Hale, (Commodore's Clerk,) United States steamer Pawnee. (This is the individual who decamped with the signal books, while Commodore Dupont's fleet rendezvoused at Hampton Roads.)

Wm. Hooper, private, Company K, Thirty-eighth New York Volunteers.

Barron Von Flaxhousen, Lieutenant, Company H, Forty-fifth New York Volunteers.

Robert McFarlans, Corporal, Company D, First United States Artillery.

A. F. Saulsbury, private, Fourth Regiment, Maine.

M. F. Sidlinger, Corporal, Company H, Fourth Regiment, Maine.

Francis Tapoy, private, Company D, First United States Artillery.

Mathias Spoo, musician, Fifth Wisconsin.

J. Tompkins, Lieutenant, Company A, Second Cavalry, United States Army.

Respecting the facilities for mail delivery to the prisoners, I feel constrained to record a fact which was highly creditable to the sympathetic feelings of the Union officers, and correspondingly to the discredit of the Confederate authorities. At one period, some three hundred letters, addressed to the Union prisoners, had accumulated at the post office, and were withheld from their owners nearly a fortnight. As soon as the Union officers were made aware of the fact, they inquired into the cause, and were informed that the post office authorities declined to deliver them until the postage was paid, and as they believed that but few of the privates had any pecuniary means, they had determined to withhold them. Upon this explanation, the Union officers directed that the letters should be delivered forthwith, and they would pay the postage, which amounted to some $25. The Confederate authorities invariably exacted seven cents per letter on delivery at the prison, notwithstanding that the five cents Confederate postage had been *pre paid* by the writers in an enclosure to Gen. Wool.

While upon this subject I may state that the receipt of letters addressed to prisoners who had died from the effects of their wounds, or from disease, was no uncommon occurrence. Such , letters were usually delivered to the acquaintances or comrades of the deceased, and they in return notified their friends of the facts.

I remember upon one occasion having heard read a letter addressed by a wife to her husband, a Philadelphian and an officer. He was one of the prisoners taken at Ball's Bluff and she had heard of his capture but not of his subsequent decease. In this letter she congratulated him upon his safety, urging upon him to keep up his spirits, and encouraging him in the hope of speedy restoration to home and friends. Alas! the returning mail conveyed to her the terrible tidings of his death.

Upon the day of this occurrence the wife of Adjutant Harvey, of the lamented Colonel Baker's Regiment, arrived in Richmond from Philadelphia. She came to the officers' quarters with joyful anticipation, and inquired for her husband. He was not there. "Not there? Strange!" She called for Lieut. Hooper, whom she knew, and in a few moments he presented himself. They exchanged but a single glance, and her countenance fell—the worst was known! She had come there with a positive conviction that her husband was alive and well. He was known to have been unwounded in the battle, and was so reported by some who had made their escape. But here ended the mystery. The Adjutant had plunged into the Potomac and was endeavoring to swim across, when he was pierced by a rebel bullet, and with scores of others, his lifeless body was carried away by the stream. Lieut. Hooper had been an eye-witness to the occurrence. No words can depict the anguish which this reluctant story drew from the broken-hearted wife. Yet she was but one among scores to whom the intelligence of the death of a beloved husband, a son, or a brother, was imparted, under circumstances perhaps as acutely distressing and insupportable.

Being deprived of frequent and regular communication with friends in the Northern States, we were compelled to rely upon the Richmond press for all political intelligence. Papers were usually brought to the prison every morning, and were purchased by the officers of the guard and handed to the prisoners at a cost of five cents per copy. Sometimes the papers, like the rations, were stinted or cut off, for misbehavior. The Richmond Dispatch was most in request on account of its peculiar bitter and vindictive course towards the prisoners called the "Yankee Government." It thus at times afforded us considerable amusement. It was a somewhat remarkable circumstance that the rebel newspaper reports of every engagement, gave evidence that the brilliant and successful fighting was all on their own side. The Yankees invariably "ran in Bull Run style," and the stereotyped commentary was in effect that running was the only thing at which "Yankees could not be beat."

It was surprising to us to learn what frightful sacrifices of life were incurred by the Federals, and how astonishingly small was the mortuary record of the Confederates. It was seldom that anybody was "hurt" on the rebel side. We did hear of an unusually severe loss having occurred to a small body of troops in Western Virginia, under Floyd, who were attacked by a largely superior force of Yankees, numbering at least ten to one. Two or three of the rebels were actually killed, and some five or six others slightly wounded. But the Yankees were terribly cut up, and retreated with heavy loss. Although victorious, (continued the report,) Floyd had deemed it a "military necessity" to fall back; but the fact that he neglected to take some of his military stores, tents, etc., was not till sometime afterwards divulged, and it is not improbable that a large proportion of the Confederate army are still in blissful ignorance of that circumstance.

I remember once reading in the Dispatch, a report of a "slight skirmish" at Drainsville. The Confederates, as usual, were attacked by overwhelming numbers, but nobly stood their ground, and caused an incalculable number of Yankees to "bite the dust." Then, as usual, the Confederates "fell back to a better position," to await another attack. It is needless to say that such transparent falsehoods could not impose upon the "Yankee" prisoners, but they were devoured with avidity and full credulity by the rebel soldiers; or at least, by such of them as could *read*.

The latter remark is in no sense ironical. Our guards were often composed of men who could *not* read, and of men who confessed to me that a large proportion of the Confederate soldiers were afflicted with the same intellectual infirmity. There was, therefore, no striking absurdity in the publication of such reports, which, however greatly exaggerated at first hands, evidently lost nothing by repetition among the pitiably ignorant and vulgar.

CHAPTER XIII.

The Confederate Shinplaster Currency had its origin in the necessity to which the business community was reduced for "making change." Union men and speculators had bought up all of the Federal coin, and it became indispensable that something of a representative value, in denominations suited to small business transactions, should be issued as a substitute. The rebel Congress was thus constrained to offer a shinplaster system, and the way was virtually opened to individuals as well as corporations. As a consequence, Richmond was soon flooded with a coarsely executed and worthless scrip, in denominations varying from five cents to one dollar. The formula of these shinplasters, as nearly as I can recollect, was about as follows. I should, perhaps, apologise for not having preserved so notable a curiosity, but the fact was that my private exchequer was so astonshingly low at the time of my departure from Richmond that, even were I so disposed, I could not have negotiated the most "vulgar fraction." Here is a sample shinplaster:

> **FIVE CENTS.**   **FIVE CENTS.**
>
> On demand I promise to pay the Bearer the sum of Five Cents, in *Bailed Hay or Groceries;* or in *Specie*, when presented in sums of *Five Dollars*, six months after a Treaty of Peace with the United States.
> [Date.]   (Signed.)   JOHN DOE.

This description of article was in unlimited supply, and when not positively known to be worthless, answered the desired purpose, in relieving the specie "rampage."

The officers, mostly, were in occasional receipt of remittances from the North, in gold, but in making their purchases, were required to accept of the inevitable shinplaster in change.

I may appropriately state in this connection, that among the prisoners was a member of the Brooklyn 14th, and who was formerly employed by the Union Bank Note Engraving Company. He was a superior engraver, and received frequent personal applications from Richmond bankers to furnish bank note engravings, or plates. One individual offered him fifteen dollars per day for four days' time, the period requisite for accomplishing the work proposed, and also to secure his release at the expiration of that time.

The engraver, however, declined the offer, and shortly afterwards made his escape from the prison. I did not learn whether he was recaptured.

Many offers of a similar character were made by manufacturers in Richmond to various mechanics in the prison, viz: shoemakers, carpenters, moulders. The most tempting prices were offered, including good board, clothes, etc., totether with a promise to send them North in a few weeks—but these applications, so far as I am informed, were invariably unsuccessful. Notwithstanding the privations to which they had been subjected, and the apparent indifference of the Federal Government, and the painful uncertainty which hung over the future, the prisoners were unwilling to purchase any personal advantage at the sacrfice of their loyalty and honor.

The Presidential election in the "Confederacy" took place on the 7th of November. It was a day of remarkable quiet. No popular demonstrations occurred—there were neither speeches nor hurrahs during the day, nor bonfires nor pyrotechnics at night. Mr. Davis was duly elected, and retained his place as Chief Magistrate of the "young and vigorous Confederacy."

On the 10th of November Gen. Winder entered the prison, called the commissioned officers together, and read the following order, as addressed to himself:

> C. S. A. WAR DEPARTMENT, }
> RICHMOND, Nov., 1861. }

SIR:—You are hereby instructed to choose by lot, from among the prisoners of war of highest rank, one who is to be confined in a cell appropriated to convicted felons, and who is to be treated in all respects as if such convict, and to be held for execution in the same manner as may be adopted by the enemy, for the execution of the prisoner of war Smith, recently condemned to death in Philadelphia.

You will also select thirteen other prisoners of war, the highest in rank of those captured by our forces, to be confined in cells reserved for prisoners accused of infamous crimes, and shall treat them as such so long as the enemy shall continue to treat the like number of prisoners of war captured by them in New York, as pirates. As these measures are intended to repress the infamous attempt now made by the enemy to commit judicial murder on the prisoners of war, you will execute them strictly, as the best mode calculated to prevent the commission of so heinous a crime.   Your obedient servant,

J. P. BENJAMIN, Acting Sec'y of War.
To Brig. General John Winder, Richmond, Va.

The reading of this order was listened to in silence, but with deep sensation. At its conclusion, Gen. Winder remarked that he regretted very much the unpleasant duty devolving upon him, but had no option in the matter. The names of six Colonels were placed in a can, and Mr. Ely was required (much to his own reluctance) to draw from them. The first name drawn was that of Colonel Corcoran, 69th Regiment N. Y. S. M., who was the hostage chosen to answer for Smith. Mr. Ely was very much affected when the name of his friend and messmate was drawn by his own hand.

In choosing thirteen, from the highest rank, to be held to answer for a like number of prisoners of war captured by the enemy at sea, there being only ten field officers, it was necessary to draw by lot three Captains.

During the drawing, the most profound silence prevailed, and great anxiety was exhibited on the part of the officers whose names were in the can. When completed, the list stood, Colonels Corcoran, Lee, Cogswell, Wilcox, Woodruff and Wood; Lieut. Colonels Mowman and Neff; Majors Potter, Revere and Vodges; Captains Rockwood, Bowman and Kaffer.

These unfortunate men had greatly endeared themselves to their fellow prisoners, and the deepest sympathy was expressed for

them. Col. Corcoran had previously been removed. His rela-
tions with Mr. Ely had been of the most intimate character, and
the latter most keenly regretted his own involuntary share in the
proceeding. It was a day of unusual gloom to those who were
left behind, but there was a confident expression that the Federal
Government would immediately take measures for the relief of
those held as hostages.

I find upon reference to my diary that the 15th of November
was observed as a day of fasting and prayer in the "Confederacy." There were religious services in all of the Richmond
churches, but I doubt whether it was considered expedient to
require any unusual "fast" among the soldiers. In respect of
"preying," it had also been practiced to an undue extent upon
the resources of all who were identified with the cause of the
Union.

On the 21st of November, twenty officers and one hundred
and twenty-five privates were sent to Tuscaloosa; and on the 26th
three hundred and fifty additional privates, including George
Rosenberg and Henry Blackman of Rochester, were despatched
to the same place. These deductions left only about twenty-five
prisoners upon the upper floors of Prison No. 1.

Christmas was commemorated in the officers' quarters by a
substantial banquet, at their own expense, and the best that could
be procured. The guard upon that occasion got rather mellow
from frequent and excessive libations, and in the evening he was
readily induced to go out after liquor, and permit one of the
officers to stand guard in his place. Some of the prisoners improved this opportunity to leave the prison and stroll about the
city, and the day following they were placed in irons as a penalty.
I had improved the occasion during the day, to slip by the guard,
but after walking a short time about the streets, perceived myself
watched by Commissary Warner and thought proper to return
without due loss of time.

On the 20th of December, Mr. Faulkner called upon Mr. Ely,
and soon after Gen. Winder entered with an order for Mr. Ely's
release. During his conversation with the officers, Mr. Faulkner
expressed his mortification at the general ill-treatment of the
Union prisoners, and promised to exert himself in procuring a
change for the better. He confessed that the rebel prisoners at
Fort Lafayette and elsewhere had nothing to complain of in
respect of fare or clothing. Mr. Ely was naturally overjoyed at
his release, but remained in Richmond till the night of the 24th.
He frequently visited the prison during the interval, and on the
24th made an affecting farewell speech to his old companions, in
which he engaged to use his utmost efforts on reaching Washington to secure their release. I believe that he has faithfully and

diligently labored to that end since he returned to Washington, and bids fair to accomplish the desired result.

About the 1st of January, the officer who called the roll selected a number of names, for the purpose, as we apprehended, of being sent South. It soon transpired, however, that the prisoners whose names were thus selected were of two hundred and forty who were to be exchanged. My own name had been omitted from the list, but Lieuts. Parke and Booth kindly interested themselves in my behalf, and greatly to my satisfaction the "mistake" was rectified in time. Subsequently Lieut. Booth offered me the sum of $300 if I would permit him to answer to my name, and clandestinely go in my place. Lieut. Hancock said to me that he had been eight months in the Federal service, and had drawn no portion of his salary, and that if I would consent to his substitution, in the manner before suggested, he would assign to me his entire claim upon the Federal Government. It is needless to say that I declined these generous offers, and I seriously doubt whether any prisoner, officer or private, would have resigned his chances for an immediate release, for the most tempting recompense imaginable.

At 5½ o'clock A. M. on the 3d of January the released prisoners marched to the river landing, and embarked on the rebel steamboat Northampton, and proceeded down the James River. At 4 P. M. we met the steamer George Washington, near Newport News, and amid the most enthusiastic shouts, cheers, and other demonstrations of rejoicing, were transferred to her decks, where for the first time since the memorable 21st of July we found ourselves beneath the folds of the STARS AND STRIPES.

CHAPTER XIV.

[With the concluding chapter of this narrative it was thought proper to insert a few letters written subsequent to the release of prisoners, which occurred on the 3d of January, together with an account of the arrival of prisoners belonging in Rochester. The articles are severally taken from the Evening Express.—ED.]

ARRIVAL IN BALTIMORE.

BALTIMORE, January 4th, 1862.

DEAR EXPRESS:—I hasten to inform you that I am *free*. I assure you that to-day is a happy one, not only to myself, but to some two hundred and fifty other unfortunates. You may imagine our joy when we received our release and were informed that we would be sent North immediately. Nearly six long, weary months have we spent in prison, subjected to many insults from the miserable tyrants who had charge of us. No pen can describe the miserable life we have spent in that rebel city of Richmond.

Thank God, we are at last here; but there are hundreds of our noble suffering comrades still incarcerated within gloomy Southern walls. I shall remain in Washington for a few days to plead for them. God grant that these poor fellows may soon be restored to the land of the *free.*

We left Richmond Tuesday morning at six o'clock in the rebel steamer Northampton. At 4 o'clock P. M. the Federal steamer George Washington met us, and received us with cheers and stirring strains of music. It is impossible to describe the scene of joy manifested at that time. As soon as *our* boat came in sight the Yankee Band struck up "Home, sweet home." When this dear old tune reached our ears, and our eyes rested upon the good old flag, which we had not seen for more than five months, we could not restrain our feelings; some danced, others sang, and such a scene of delight I never before witnessed. Many tears of joy were shed when we looked up to that noble old flag. For my own part, I felt like kissing it! We were kindly and cordially received by our own officers, and were soon on our way to Fortress Monroe, which place we reached at six o'clock the same evening. We were received with great rejoicing at every place we stopped, and were received by the citizens with unlimited hospitality. We were escorted to a large building which the fair ladies of Baltimore had elevated, and where we were furnished with a sumptuous repast. It is hardly necessary to say that we did ample justice to the collation, after five months of fasting. We expect to leave for Washington this afternoon. A large crowd of visitors have been in and about the building all day, and the boys have had a happy time since they arrived on Northern soil. The Union sentiment is very strong in this city, in fact the good people of Baltimore are all alive with enthusiasm, and ready for the worst. It will be some weeks yet before any of the released prisoners are fit for duty. All are enervated by long confinement and feel the cold very severely.

More anon. W. H. M.

BALTIMORE, January 7th, 1862.

DEAR EXPRESS:—We are still detained in this city awaiting orders from Washington. The War Department has not yet decided what disposition to make of us. It is rumored that we are to be mustered out of service and turned over to the Governors of our respective States. I hope there is no foundation for this rumor, as such action would place us in other regiments, which would be very unpleasant to many, and is inexpedient.

I hope the Administration will continue to send prisoners forward, to be exchanged, until all of our poor, suffering volunteers are released. I am glad that there is so good a prospect of such a policy being carried out. There is a strong feeling in this city

on the subject.   The Confederate authorities will not fail to reciprocate, as they are very anxious to get rid of Yankees, for they
are a very expensive and troublesome burthen to them.   The
meat bill, alone, for the prisoners in Richmond amounts to over
$9,000 a month.   I wish I could have sent you some of their
editorials on this subject.   They had all they could do to get men
enough to guard us.   I will give you some interesting items in
this respect when I return.

It would be a good idea to get our poor fellows home, and
form them into regiments by themselves, and give them the right
of the line in the next great battle.   If they would not make
the rebels bite the dust, it would be because they could out-run
them.   The boys have *several* small accounts to settle with the
Southern (bogus) Confederacy and *a few deaths to avenge.*   It
would have been better by far for our enemies to have sent us
home as soon as we were able to leave the hospital.   They were
very kind to us *there* and we all felt like praising them for their
attention.   But this mode of treatment soon changed, and they
went to the opposite extreme, and became as brutal as they had
been kind.   I was told by one of the officers that they did intend to heal our wounds, load us with obligations and then send
us home to tell our Northern friends how noble and kind the
Southerners were.   But this policy was abandoned.   No pen can
describe the true condition of our brave soldiers confined in rebel
prisons.   Their sufferings have been, and are great.   God be with
them.   I will give you a full account of our condition and treatment before many days.   I am too happy, at present, to write.
The idea of being free, and once more standing under the
dear old flag, is enough to make us all rejoice, after having spent
so many weary months in prison, and looking at the hybrid rag
which they call their banner of freedom.   I have a secesh flag
with me, presented by the daughter of the rebel Major Lee.   I
feel a lasting, if not a tender regard for it, I assure you.   I learn
that the citizens of Philadelphia expect a visit from the prisoners
and are making preparations to receive them.   W. H. M.

THE RECEPTION BY SLOCUM'S BRIGADE.

CAMP FRANKLIN, Jan. 13, 1862.
FRIEND B.:—On Saturday last the prisoners arrived from
Richmond.   For a day or two previous all was bustle in camp,
making preparations for their reception.   The streets were fes-
tooned with evergreens, and wreaths containing the letter of each
company in the center.   A triumphal arch was erected on the
extreme left of the street, between the officers' and companies'
quarters.   On the left of the arch, within a wreath, was the number of the Regiment, (27,) and in the center the following:

WELCOME, COMRADES!

YOUR WOUNDS BLEED AFRESH IN OUR HEARTS.

At three o'clock, Saturday afternoon, the whole Regiment turned out and, preceded by Scott's Band, and accompanied by General Slocum and staff, proceeded down the Alexandria Road about three-quarters of a mile, where they halted and formed in open order, facing inward. Gen. Slocum and staff, together with the Regimental officers, then advanced to receive the prisoners, and escort them through the ranks. The command of the prisoners was given to your Richmond correspondent, Corporal Merrell, and when they started, a scene of excitement ensued which baffles description. The cheering could be heard for miles. It did not end here, for it was taken up by the several Regiments encamped near us, and continued long after the arrival of our comrades in camp. Scott's Band played the "Bold Soger Boy," and the band of another Regiment struck up a piece entitled "Bully for You!"

The men look as though they had seen "hard times in Old Virginia," although some of them appear quite stout. But it is not healthy flesh. It is what physicians call "lazy bloat," induced by protracted confinement. Corporal Merrell looks well, but is very pale. His left arm is nearly powerless. I understand that he has been offered a commission, and that he will accept it. If such be the case, he will be heartily welcomed as an officer of the 27th. He has proved himself a brave soldier, and is possessed, I think, of qualifications which should entitle him to a command. But he is willing to undergo the same suffering again, "for the sake of" (as he expressed himself to me) "the good old flag."

Clague carries the ball he received in the left side. He says it does not trouble him any. He is undaunted by the fearful ordeal through which he has passed ; so far from it, indeed, that he had some hesitancy about accepting the thirty days' furlough. He says it is his intention to rejoin the regiment as soon as his furlough expires.

Of the other prisoners I have not much knowledge. They were all highly gratified at the reception given them by their old companions-in-arms, who were equally rejoiced at the opportunity of once more beholding them alive and well.　＊　＊　＊　＊

DUNCAN B. BROWN.

RETURN OF RICHMOND PRISONERS—AN IMPROMTU DEMONSTRATION.

Messrs. Merrell, Clague and Kavanaugh, late of Richmond, arrived in Rochester last evening, (January 17th.) A large crowd were in waiting at the Depot, on the arrival of the train from Elmira, and several fire companies were drawn up in line to

receive them. The appearance of the "prisoners," as they are
still called, was greeted with resounding cheers, and after the
enthusiasm of welcome had in some measure subsided, they were
formally escorted to the residence of Corporal Merrell on New
Main street—the procession greatly augmenting its number *en
route.*   •

On reaching their destination the prisoners entered the house,
where many friends were in waiting ; but they were quickly
brought out again by three rousing cheers from the crowd, on
behalf of whom Mr. G. C. Pease delivered a brief and appropriate
address of welcome to the soldiers, referring to the gallantry which
had characterized their behavior at Bull Run, commending the
heroic fortitude which they had manifested under protracted imprisonment at Richmond, and, finally, congratulating them upon
their restoration to home and friends.

Corporal Merrell modestly acknowledged the compliment of a
popular reception, disclaiming any personal merit, beyond that
which should be accorded to every faithful soldier in the Union
army, but testifying to the bravery of his comrades, and the Regiment to which they are attached, (the 27th.) He alluded feel-
ingly to the sufferings they had experienced during their imprisonment, at the hands of their heartless and cruel captors, and
hinted at the determination of the prisoners generally to rejoin
the army, after a brief season of repose.

At the conclusion of his remarks three cheers were given, and
then "three cheers and a tiger." The company then fell in line,
and escorted private John T. Clague to his residence on Clinton
street, where brief speeches were again exchanged, and the company returned to their engine house.

The effect of a long imprisonment is quite visible in the pale
faces of the prisoners, and the enervation resulting from bodily
inaction. Private Kavanagh will leave to-day for Detroit, where
his parents reside.

The gallant John Clague, who was *obituarized* by his Sabbath
School, and *resolved* under the "sacred soil" of Virginia with all
due solemnity, exhibits the honorable scars of wounds from which
he has not yet fully recovered, but is none the less anxious to
resume his place in the ranks.

Kelly, Sturmer, Jewett, Cornell, each and every one of the
brave fellows released from Southern bondage, are not only willing but fully determined, we are assured, to re-enter the Union
army, not only to fight for the *Union*, but to avenge the wicked
cruelties inflicted upon themselves and comrades.

Corporal Merrell has a thirty days' furlough which he accepted
in lieu of a discharge tendered him at Washington. He has not
fully recovered from the effect of his wound, being still unable to
use his left arm with freedom.

ROCHESTER CALORIC PRINTING OFFICE.

BENTON & ANDREWS,

𝔅𝔬𝔬𝔨 𝔞𝔫𝔡 𝔍𝔬𝔟 ℜ𝔯𝔦𝔫𝔱𝔢𝔯𝔰,

DEALERS IN STATIONERY, AND

PUBLISHERS OF LAW BLANKS,

Over 29 Buffalo Street, - - **Rochester, N. Y.**

Having taken the second story of the building occupied by us, and refitted our office, adding to our facilities for Plain and Ornamental Printing, we feel confident of giving good satisfaction to all who favor us with their patronage. Our facilities for printing

CASES AND POINTS,

PAMPHLETS, CIRCULARS, BILL-HEADS,

Letter-Heads, Cards, Etc., are Unsurpassed.

We have recently made arrangements with F. H. MARSHALL, the well-known

Plain and Ornamental Book Binder,

To remove his Bindery into the building with us, by which our facilities for getting up

RECORD BOOKS, FOR COUNTY OFFICERS,

CHECK BOOKS, DRAFT BOOKS,

BLANK BOOKS FOR BANKS, ETC.,

are greatly increased.

By attention to business, we intend to deserve a share of patronage. We rely upon the superiority of our work, instead of political organizations, for the favor of the public.

Remember the place,

No. 29 BUFFALO STREET,

Nearly opposite the Arcade.

JAMES W. BENTON, }
EZRA R. ANDREWS. }   ROCHESTER, N. Y.

5

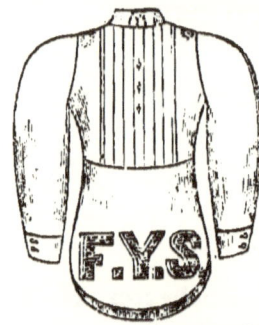

ESTABLISHMENT MITCHELL.

WM. L. MARKELL & BRO.

Manufacturers and Wholesale Dealers in

MITCHELL'S GENUINE

PERFUMERY,

FLAVORING EXTRACTS, &c.

69 State Street,   -   -   Rochester, N. Y.

MITCHELL'S GOODS

Are the Best and Most Reliable in the World,

BE SURE AND

BUY NONE BUT THE GENUINE.

Owing to the universally acknowledged superiority of all Goods
issued by this House, many worthless imitations and
counterfeits are to be found in the market.

All Articles Emanating from this Establishment are

PREPARED BY THE INVENTOR,

D. MITCHELL,

EACH PACKAGE BEARING HIS WRITTEN SIGNATURE.

AND THEY, ONLY, ARE GENUINE.

☞ Orders to this House will be promptly attended to. ☜

www.ingramcontent.com/pod-product-compliance
Lightning Source LLC
Chambersburg PA
CBHW030009030726
47499CB00008B/2976